D0706266

PRAISE FOR
THE RETAIL CHAMPION

This book has so many 'golden ~~eggs~~ ... ~~names and tips~~ especially for new start-ups. It would certainly have been one of the most thumbed books on my desk!! Well worth the read.

Mike Clare, Founder and President of Dreams plc

Don't start up a retail business until you have read this book!

Hussein Lalani, Co-Founder, 99p Stores

Clare has been a real champion of independent retailers and her book provides the sort of vital insights they need to help them compete in today's punishing trading conditions.

George MacDonald, Deputy Editor, *Retail Week*

This book really is the 'one-stop shop' stocking everything retailers and would-be retailers need to create, establish and grow a successful retail business.

Ben Sillitoe, Editor, *Retail Gazette*

Stop playing shops! Master these 10 core steps to retail success and take control of your venture and opportunities.

**Doug Richards, Entrepreneur, Investor,
Founder of School for Startups**

Need a shot of retail caffeine to galvanize your retail business? Don't just wake up and smell the coffee, this book is a full-strength double espresso to REALLY get you going.

**Michael Weedon, Deputy Chief Executive, bira
(British Independent Retailers Association)**

Cutting it on the high street requires a great business idea AND the business know-how to make the dream happen. This book is the definitive guide to retail your way to success.

Nigel J L Rothband, Chief Executive, *Retail Trust*

A fantastic read. Excellent insight that will certainly make a difference to any retail entrepreneurs looking to succeed.

**Ian Shipman, Regional Director,
Angels Den, one of the largest global angel networks**

If you really want to make a success of your retail business, whether you've been trading for 40 years or are just in the planning stages of setting up your first shop, this is the perfect book for you. I just wish it had been around when I was starting up!

Sarah Decent, Owner, Modish Shoes

This is the must-have book for every independent retailer – an insight into the ways and means to create and sustain a successful retail business.

**Andy Laird, Managing Director of Fludes Carpets
(independent flooring retailer, founded in 1929)**

This is an independent retailer's best friend. A must-read with useful tools and techniques to be mastered and keep retail business in the high street game.

**Kerry Bannigan, Co-Founder of Nolcha
and Independent Retailer Month**

Implement Clare's '10 steps to retail success' and make your business boom!

Thomas Power, Chairman of Ecademy

The Retail Champion

The Retail Champion

10 steps to retail success

Clare Rayner

KoganPage

LONDON PHILADELPHIA NEW DELHI

First published in Great Britain and the United States in 2012 by Kogan Page Limited

120 Pentonville Road
London N1 9JN
United Kingdom
www.koganpage.com

1518 Walnut Street, Suite 1100
Philadelphia PA 19102
USA

4737/23 Ansari Road
Daryaganj
New Delhi 110002
India

© Clare Rayner, 2012

The right of Clare Rayner to be identified as the author of this work has been asserted by her in accordance with the Copyright, Designs and Patents Act 1988.

ISBN   978 0 7494 6588 9
E-ISBN   978 0 7494 6589 6

British Library Cataloguing-in-Publication Data

A CIP record for this book is available from the British Library.

Library of Congress Cataloging-in-Publication Data

Rayner, Clare.
    The retail champion : 10 steps to retail success / Clare Rayner.
        p. cm.
    Includes index.
    ISBN 978-0-7494-6588-9 – ISBN 978-0-7494-6589-6 (ebook)   1. Retail trade–Management.
2. Small business–Management.   I. Title.
    HF5429.R345 2012
    658.8'7–dc23
                                                                                                2012007724

Typeset by Graphicraft Ltd, Hong Kong
Printed and bound in India by Replika Press Pvt Ltd

CONTENTS

ACKNOWLEDGEMENTS

In advance of the body of this book I wanted to take some time to thank those who have been instrumental in it coming to fruition, and to share a little as to how they have contributed.

Andrew Rayner: My husband, business partner, supporter, sounding board and critic! His support for my personal goals and his contribution to our business goals have enabled me to achieve what I set out to do.

My family: If they'd not been entrepreneurs, business owners and retailers I wouldn't be in the position I am in today, knowing what I know, doing what I love.

Mike Clare: For being an amazing role model for any small retailer. For giving up his time to write the foreword for this book; for letting me interview him and for believing in me.

Sarah Decent: Sarah sowed the seed for this book! If she hadn't tweeted for help with her retail business, or asked where to find a book on 'how to become a successful retailer', it may have been a good deal longer before I actually got around to writing it!

Sue Blake: I 'discovered' Sue thanks to my friend Emma Wimhurst who also sang her praises in HER book! Initially Sue helped me to clarify and articulate the core purpose for *The Retail Champion*. Latterly she has been a fantastic support, mentor and friend.

Wanda Whitely: I was introduced to Wanda by Sue. Wanda is an ex-publishing director who now advises authors on everything from creating a proposal to negotiating a contract. Wanda helped me to write the outline proposal for this book. Wanda and Sue together gave me the belief that this book not only should be written, but also deserved a mainstream publisher to bring it to market!

Martina O'Sullivan: With Sue and Wanda encouraging me, I connected with Martina on LinkedIn. Her role as commissioning editor for Kogan Page, a publisher Sue had identified as ideal for my book, meant she was obviously a connection I needed to make. Within 20 minutes of accepting my invitation to connect, Martina had browsed my profile and noticed I had stated that I was writing my first business book. After a brief exchange of e-mails I sent her the proposal that Wanda had helped me to craft. Two hours later we'd booked a lunch meeting. Martina was the perfect connection and so in tune with what I wanted for this book. After that lunch meeting we both agreed that we should work together; and so my relationship with Kogan Page began. Martina has been there every step of the way; I may know a lot about retail but I knew nothing about the process of writing a book. She has been a guide and a supporter – I've loved working with her. She's also proven that it doesn't have to be painful to get published!

Jacqueline Gold, Hussein Lalani, Nigel Rothband, Natalie Peters, Sadia Sisay: Thanks to all of you for allowing me to include your stories as case studies in this book.

FOREWORD

I first met Clare Rayner in 2007 when we were both invited to speak to a group of enthusiastic 14- to 21-year-olds. The event was a government-led initiative to engage and inspire the next generation of employees and entrepreneurs. Our purpose was to prove just how rewarding and diverse a career in retail could be.

Clare spoke about her passion and enthusiasm in building a business. The title was 'From flippin' burgers to 'flippin' busy' – aimed perfectly at the audience of sceptical teenagers! She explained her career from working part-time in McDonald's, her progression, the different facets of retailing and so on. The teenage audience started to take notice. Clare made retailing sound exciting, fun and rewarding.

I was impressed by her passion, enthusiasm and knowledge of the retail industry. Since starting Dreams in 1985, I'd not met many people who had covered so many of the core elements essential to the running of a retail business – from store operations to supply-chain management, commercial planning to business systems implementation.

In 2007, Clare had been running her own business for four years, having started out at a similar age to me when I set up Dreams. Her entrepreneurial spirit has been proven over the years as she has developed new brands and business ventures. In 2008 I spoke at her annual event, The Retail Conference, in London, which was a well-orchestrated event, relevant to the audience of retail delegates.

Now, once again, I have had the pleasure of contributing to one of her projects. *The Retail Champion* is a comprehensive guide to successful retailing. The 10-steps methodology provides a structure and process that are so easy to use by both established retailers and start-up retailers.

With each step building on the previous one, the outcome is a powerful overview of where a business owner really needs to focus their efforts to take their business to the next level.

Clare's style is conversational, supportive and open – this book is easy to read, enjoyable and a tool that can be used again and again by a business owner to review, refresh and further develop their retail brand.

The advice to develop robust and repeatable processes and sytems to deliver a scalable enterprise is succinct and true. I think it is fair to say that had this book been available to me when I was starting out, I believe I would have achieved every milestone successfully, far quicker, with greater confidence and possibly with fewer mistakes!

So, whether you are an established retailer or just thinking of starting up a retail business, my advice is to invest some time to work through this book – you will undoubtedly benefit from it!

Good luck and may all your 'Dreams' come true!

Mike Clare, Founder and President of Dreams plc

Introduction

My aim

First of all thank you for choosing to read this book. I hope you enjoy it. The aim of this book is to help more retail business owners, whether starting up or already trading, online only or multi-channel, to develop robust and repeatable processes and systems to create scalable, saleable enterprises.

When I work with clients 1-2-1 on mentoring programmes this is what we set out to achieve. We do so by working through '10 steps to retail success', a process that I have developed. This book will walk you through each of those 10 steps, brought to life with lots of real-world examples, so that even if we're not able to work together 1-2-1 you can still work through each of the 10 steps. I hope that at the end of this book you will be armed with the information, confidence and motivation you need to enable you to improve your retail business and to attain your business and personal goals.

Firstly I'd like to share with you what I mean by 'develop robust and repeatable processes and systems to create a scalable, saleable enterprise' – it's a hefty statement! Working with a wonderful lady – Sue Blake – who is my visibility advisor, mentor and friend, I created this statement. Essentially this distils what I believe in, and what I deliver through the 10 steps to retail success process, into just a few words. I hope that by explaining what I believe each word means you'll have a better understanding of what to expect, and what you'll achieve as you work through this book and as you complete each of the 10 steps.

Robust: By this I mean simple, clear, easy-to-follow (one could say 'foolproof') processes that are unambiguous. Any member of staff, regardless of experience, can work 'by the book'. You've given them the operating manual.

Repeatable: obvious, really – meaning your robust processes can be done to a consistent standard, time and again, replicating what your customers have come to expect from you.

Processes and systems: these are the day-to-day actions, interactions, transactions and analysis your business needs to be doing to operate and deliver on your customer promise. These are done by either your people or are automated: done by computer processors. This includes anything from setting up a new product on the till to handling a customer complaint.

Scalable: This is very important; it's about utilizing the robust and repeatable processes that you've created so that you can grow your business without YOU becoming a bottleneck! When you're a scalable business you're able to walk away having delegated to others, and you'll have the confidence that the business will operate effectively, and to your standards, without you.

Saleable: The ultimate endorsement of your success – your business has a value in the eyes of an outsider. In order to realize the very best value for your business, should you choose to move on, it needs to have the previous three ingredients. A potential buyer will recognize the value of your business only when you can prove that the business is scalable, and that it can grow. To sell your business you need a new owner to be confident that with new management in place everything you've built will continue to thrive without you at the helm.

Good luck with your journey – at the end of this introduction I've included a self-appraisal sheet for you to complete. This should be a brutally honest assessment of where you are and where you feel you ought to be in terms of the 10 steps. This will help you identify the areas where you need most work, and the areas where you need least.

Before we get cracking, though, I thought you'd like to know what on earth made me decide to dedicate every spare minute of my life for eight weeks so that I could get all this down on paper.

Inspiration

For years my network of business connections has been telling me to write a book – but I was extremely reluctant! It wasn't the book per se that I was avoiding; for me it was about timing. I didn't want to jump on what appeared to be a book-writing bandwagon; because everywhere I looked people were self-publishing books in order to create the impression of expertise. I really disliked this approach; it was creating a mushrooming number of 'experts' who now, book in hand, were flooding the business community.

But then one day I was sent a tweet that had originated from a lady called Sarah Decent. Sarah had bought a shoe retail business, Modish, a couple of years prior and at the time traded from two shops and an e-commerce site. Sarah had turned to Twitter in her frustration at not being able to find what she was looking for; her tweet read something like this: 'Help me. Where can I find a book to help me run my retail business properly? I need to stop playing shops!'

So I answered her. I said: 'I guess I really do need to write one; but as that's a bit of a way off, why don't we have a chat?'

And Sarah became one of the first clients for the new brand I'd just launched, specifically dedicated to helping smaller, independent retailers – The Retail Champion.

Working with Sarah, going through the 10 steps to retail success I'd developed, I quickly realized that NOW I had relevant, useful content that made writing a book suddenly seem important.

So this book is not written as an extension of my business card or as a glorified brochure for my services. It is written in order to enable me to share the 10 steps to retail success with many more business owners than I could ever reach 1-2-1. It is something I want to be a valuable guide and reference tool for ALL smaller retailers – from start-ups to established businesses; from online only to multi-channel. My vision is that this book gets *used* and what I mean by that is that it looks tatty when you've done with it! I want to know you've had it on hand to refer to; you've covered it in notes and comments. I want to see coffee stains on the cover and markers on the pages that you like to refer back to most often. So, when you've been using your copy a while, can you share a photo with me to show me what you've done with yours? I'd love to see it!

I've poured my passion for retail and retailing into this book; I hope you enjoy it and benefit from it.

Back to Sarah, my 'inspiration': I'd like to tell you a bit more about her, her background and what she had to say when I told her that thanks to her tweet, this book would happen.

About Sarah Decent

Sarah Decent used to be the European HR director for Technicolor. In this role she was living in Rome on an 18-month secondment when she fell in love with the wealth of independent retailers in the city. This secondment was her inspiration for a whole new career. She loved the fact that chain stores didn't dominate the city, that there were still so many independent boutiques operating there, offering wonderful products and service to match. These smaller retailers coexisted in harmony with the bigger chains, making Rome a perfect shopping destination for the lucky consumers. When she came back to the UK she quit her job and bought a struggling retail business, which comprised a shoe shop and a website. Sarah was a successful professional BUT she had no experience in retailing.

After a couple of years of trying to make the business work, Sarah admitted that she was ready for help. She wanted a robust process, through which she could expand the business. She was fed up with 'playing shops'.

What Sarah Decent said

About a year ago I was struck by the sudden realization that whilst I absolutely loved owning and running my two little shoe shops I didn't really have a clue what I was doing! They were going ok, but I wanted to make them great!

Being the daughter of a librarian and a publisher I made straight to the nearest bookshop for inspiration. Surely there would be loads of books to tell me just what I should be doing to run a professional independent retail business? But to my frustration there was nothing. NOTHING AT ALL! Sure, if I would have been happy with some basic styling and window-dressing tips, then yes, that would have been catered for. And if I was studying for a degree in Retail Management and needed to find out what the national chains were up to, again I would have been fine too. But those books had very little of any relevance to a small retail operation like mine.

In frustration I turned to Twitter, more in hope than expectation: 'Help! I'm an independent retailer feeling the need to up her game rather than just play at shops. Any suggestions?'

It got a couple of re-tweets, no more. But one of them proved to be my salvation as it came to the attention of Clare Rayner, The Retail Champion, who suggested we meet up for a no-obligations chat. And what an eye-opener that was! In those two hours Clare gave me more help and useful advice than I'd gleaned in the previous two-and-a-half years! Clare was able to translate her extensive experience working for and with many of the UK's blue-chip retail conglomerates into something that will work for someone like me, with a couple of shops.

If you set up your own shop it's a very personal thing – it's your baby! Clare gets you to take a step back and look at your business with a dispassionate eye. Her step-by-step process gives you a framework which allows you to assess what it is that your business actually offers, what you hope to achieve with your business and how to make sure you actually get there! And all the advice is aimed at you – a small retailer, so you get loads of great tips, advice and guidance on critical areas such as positioning yourself in the market, pricing strategy, managing your stock and cash flow; none of which was available anywhere else.

If you really want to make a success of your business, whether you've been trading for 40 years or are just in the planning stages of setting up your first shop, this is the perfect book for you. I just wish it had been around when I was starting up!

Sarah Decent, Owner, Modish.

Why this book? Why now?

It wasn't only Sarah that got me moving on this, although she sowed the seed! What was going on in the retail market in the UK in mid-2011 (and globally), and what had been going on for the previous two years, was a sorry story. The industry was in distress – why would any entrepreneur consider creating a retail business with the seemingly unending list of businesses failing? The size and scale of the business seemed irrelevant, the carnage was indiscriminate – large and small retailers dropping like flies. In just one week at the end of June 2011 a list of four major UK retailers ALL ceased trading, adding to a 'graveyard' of retail brands that all met their bitter end due to the global economic downturn. Those still trading were announcing vast swathes of store closures to try to control their costs and respond to the drop in consumer demand. The centres of most towns in the UK, the home for a vast majority of chains and independents alike, were looking more and more like ghost towns with a record number of premises vacant. Amongst this doom and gloom, however, several retailers were doing very well, growing and flourishing – these included both discounters (such as 99p Stores) and higher-end retailers (such as Waitrose). What was the secret? Well, it seemed to be that they had a very clear proposition and that they kept their promises; you'll hear more about this in Step 2, positioning.

Still, if UK retailing was going to recover (and don't forget the UK has often been called a nation of shopkeepers) something needed to change. It's all too easy to lay blame on the rise of online shopping, on big out-of-town developments, and on supermarkets; but the blame lies firmly at the door of retailers who have had it too good for too long.

Retailers have been caught out by a step-change in consumer behaviour. In the 'boom time' they failed to innovate or prepare a resilient, agile business model that would enable them to adapt to fluctuating economic conditions and the influence that had on consumer behaviour. So when there was a fundamental shift in the market conditions, they were not able to adapt in time... like the dinosaurs, they became extinct.

With many of the long-established retailers falling prey to the global economic downturn, independents are understandably nervous; not knowing why the bigger players collapsed, wondering if they will be next. But customers must shop, they need products and welcome the social interaction and enjoyment they get from a good shopping experience.

There is money to be made in retail but you need to know how. It is my aim that this book will give smaller retailers the tools, techniques, confidence and motivation they need to not just survive the high street carnage but to thrive – to steal the march on those who have rested on their laurels for too long, and to secure the long-term loyalty of a more cautious, more considered, consumer.

Running a retail business can be tough, all-consuming and nothing like having a 'regular' job. You need to be certain that you want to do it and are ready to do it. As Hussein Lalani, co-founder of 99p Stores, said, 'Don't remortgage your house to start up a retail business until you've read this book' – essentially, if you've got any doubts this book will flush them out, and perhaps make you think again; but if you are sure you are ready then we'll work together, throughout this book, to enable you to implement robust, repeatable processes in your business so that in future you can do things like go on holiday, knowing that when you come back the business has survived without you!

My background

Nowadays I am known as The Retail Champion and I am engaged by clients as a consultant, professional speaker and business mentor as well as being regularly called upon by the BBC and trade press to comment on retail matters.

Through my main business, which I co-founded with my husband Andrew, I own and run three brands that service the retail sector:

- The Retail Conference – the UK's leading annual retail industry event that is offered FREE to all retailers.

- Retail Acumen – a retail consulting brand that offers detailed analytics and insights into business performance improvement opportunities for retail multiples.

- The Retail Champion – mentoring and consulting services for independent retail business owners.

My husband runs e-mphasis internet marketing: a digital marketing agency that specializes in providing services to clients whose customer is the consumer, typically those in retail, hospitality and leisure.

As if that wasn't enough we turned the surplus space in our own offices into a serviced and virtual office solution for local, small businesses *and* because of my husband's love of technology he's been retailing clearance business technology items since 2007 as well!

You can find out more about my business interests in the Appendix.

Of course I have had a long career path over many years that enabled me to get to this position: running a number of successful small businesses, writing this book, and sharing some of the experience from that career with you.

You might wonder what qualifies me to write this book or to advise you. You'd be right to question me, too – all too many people today are ready to claim expertise and it seems there are a lot of 'experts' who over-promise and under-deliver. I hope I'll never be one of those. In order to gain your trust I want to share some of my story with you – my family background and my retail experience – to give you confidence in me and in what I share with you in this book.

Certainly I was a child born into a family of entrepreneurs, with a retail bias dating back over 100 years. I don't recall ever NOT being involved with or surrounded by retailers – I guess it is literally in my blood.

I grew up surrounded by my family of retailers. My parents ran a successful fine furnishings business, which they sold in the 1990s to retire. For over 20 years they operated what would today be described as a multi-channel retail brand, although they predated the internet! They had several retail outlets, concessions in other stores (including a couple of major chains), a mail/telephone order catalogue and a factory shop. Rather than buying in goods to resell, their model was make to order, a bespoke service for each customer uniquely, so they additionally had full warehousing and manufacturing capabilities.

Family mealtimes were like board meetings; holidays were often the cover story told to us kids for what was in fact a trip to a fabric supplier; outings inevitably meant browsing the competition – and that meant spending a lot of time walking around both independent fabric shops and major department stores.

I didn't mind at all, though – in fact I loved it – I was lapping it all up, although I didn't realize it at the time. As soon as my handwriting was good enough I used to write addresses on envelopes to send out our catalogues and as soon as I could take a phone enquiry I helped out in the office, taking orders and helping customers.

It wasn't just my parents, though – my grandparents also had a factory and a shop, my other grandmother ran a hotel, three of my uncles had a pub, a deli and a corner shop between them, and my aunt ran a fashion boutique. My great grandfather had been an importer and wholesaler of fruit and veg, as had his father before him – and so it continues, as far up the family tree as I have attempted to trace.

As a teenager I always had a myriad of jobs, although not always for the family business (it just isn't that cool to work for your parents!). By the age of 16 I'd got a motor scooter and so in the school holidays was juggling being the only member of staff working in a served fuel station with an attached convenience store, working in my parents' showroom, doing reception in a beauty salon *and* doing quality control in the local photographic laboratory! If that wasn't enough I used to collect remnants of fabric at my parents' factory, and stray elastic bands from the bundles of postal enquiries that arrived each day, to make them up into funky 'scrunchies' (hair bands) using the sewing machines in the factory out of hours. I retailed these to fellow schoolmates for £1 an item. Not only was this a great money-spinner, I was rather ahead of my time too – 'up-cycling': creating unique fashion statements from rubbish (as the majority of my raw materials were otherwise destined to be disposed of).

When tired of my hairband empire I began to organize outings to theme parks such as Alton Towers. I'd book the coach and negotiate a group ticket price. On several occasions I was able to get a discount on the advertised group rate just because I asked! I'd work out a price point for the trip as a package that would be acceptable to my school friends based on known pocket-money rates. I'd calculate how many tickets I needed to sell to break even (to cover the fixed cost of the coach and the entry price to the park) so from that I'd know what the margin per additional sale was; thus how much money I was making on the event overall.

Yes, that entrepreneurial streak that had been in my family for over a century was part of my fabric too!

That said, I didn't immediately decide to launch my own business and follow in my family's entrepreneurial footsteps. I was attracted to the 'bright lights and big city', so moved to London. I'd spent my teenage years in the countryside long before such things as mobile phones and the internet, so I was keen to see some 'life'. Breaking the mould I tried my hand at academia and took up a place on a four-year MEng in Chemical Engineering at Imperial College in London. I'd got all the ingredients to be a first-class honours student – bar one: the desire to be on a production line education system for the next four years. My calling was to be out there earning money. So, I dropped out of university and started working. By day I was managing a luxury shoe concession in Harvey Nichols, by night I was a crew member in my local McDonald's. At about the same time I bought my first property; I was 19. In keeping with that entrepreneurial streak, I rented out the spare rooms so that the rental income covered the mortgage. Being 19, that meant that I was able to enjoy spending my salary on having a lot of fun!

I guess it was a number of things; like advertising for flatmates in the staff room, like turning up to work at McDonald's in a very smart outfit (from Harvey Nichols) and doing a quick change into my uniform that made my regional manager take notice of me. He put me on their graduate training programme – and to this day, hand on heart, it was the best 'how to run a business' course I can say I've ever had. McDonald's really empower their management – but within a clearly laid-down framework. The secret to their success is their ability to offer consistency in both service and product quality in any store around the world. It was my experience at McDonald's that cemented my belief that if a business wants to become a successful, scalable, saleable enterprise they first need to have robust, repeatable processes and systems, and that's stayed with me ever since!

It was also at McDonald's that I discovered my passion for all of the commercial and planning processes – such as how to calculate the number of bread rolls to order to meet demand, how to produce a forecast, how all of the orders got aggregated across all the stores, etc. I was intrigued as to how those orders were communicated daily to the suppliers and in turn how that enabled them to plan their raw materials and manufacturing.

I loved the intricacies of the 'system' of the supply chain. I was fascinated by how each and every operator, in every store, was integral to the whole 'machine' and its ability to effectively function, profitably, as planned.

There were no opportunities for me to explore this fascination with the end-to-end supply chain with McDonald's HQ and so, in my quest to learn, I left McDonald's to join M&S head office as a 'graduate' trainee. This was my first head office job – from there I moved around various retailers, taking career advancement opportunities and experiencing all aspects of the business, and in particular commercial planning aspects, which armed me with the skills and experience I have today. You can read all about what I've done on my LinkedIn profile – **www.linkedin.com/in/clarerayner**.

I am sure I could fill this whole book telling stories about McDonald's, M&S and all the other retailers I've worked for – but I am not sure that would meet my aim: to share with you how you can implement 10 steps to retail success, to 'stop playing shops' as Sarah Decent put it.

Introducing the 10 steps to retail success

The 10 steps to retail success are not complex – we're talking about serving consumers, *not* solving world famine! To develop business processes that are right for *your* retail brand takes trial and error, testing and refining. Once you've got a result you are happy with, it needs strong leadership to communicate and excellent management to control. Most importantly, to avoid being a victim of economic conditions and shifts in consumer behaviour, it needs constant re-evaluation and revision where appropriate. It's a continuous improvement process – you always need to be checking back that what you offer is still relevant, still appropriate and moving with the times. Don't rest on your laurels and get left behind.

I believe that these 10 steps will give you the tools and techniques you need to not only improve your business now but also to undertake that ongoing evaluation process in the future. You can use them time and time again, and with each iteration you'll be taking your business forward, refining it, finessing it and future-proofing it.

By now you should be fired up and ready to get started. Ahead of Step 1 I promised I'd share the 10 steps to retail success self-appraisal tool, which will form the basis for your action plan. This is outlined in full below. All I want you to do now, ahead of Step 1, is to complete the 'current position' column. If you prefer to keep a soft copy then you can download this template as an Excel spreadsheet template via **www.retailchampion.co.uk/ resources** – it's called '10-steps to retail success self-appraisal'. Being in Excel means that you can sort/filter columns on things like priority, cost or due date.

Access to the resources area is usually exclusively offered to my clients, but I've decided to open it up to all those who read this book. The first time you visit the resources page you will need to complete the form on the right, including the access code from the front of this book, to request your log-in PIN. As soon as you are issued with your PIN you will gain the same level of access as any of my clients, free of charge. With this you will be able to download a variety of tools, templates and calculators that are mentioned throughout this book.

As you complete each of the 10 steps, take some time to think about what your target position should be, relative to that step, and then complete the target position column of your self-appraisal tool. When you've done that, looking at where you are and where you want to be, think about the actions required to get you to your target position. Make a note of those actions so that throughout your progress through each of the 10 steps you are building up your overall action plan.

As I mentioned, we'll come back to this self-appraisal tool when we reach the conclusion of this book. We'll look at how to take the list of actions required to reach your target position, and will develop those into a fully costed, prioritized action plan for your business.

Let's get started!

TABLE 0.1 10 steps to retail success self-appraisal tool

Step & short description	Current position	Target position	Actions required	Dependent actions	Priority: H/M/L	Cost estimate	Due date
1. Goal and mission: Has clearly defined goal and mission statement							
2. Positioning: Has determined positioning in respect of product, price, presentation and service							
3. Ideal customer: Has clearly documented ideal customer for each range planned							
4. Range planning: Has a clearly documented approach to range construction, width vs depth and it matches the mission, positioning and customer needs							
5. Pricing and promotions: Has a price architecture, price ladder and promotional approach that fits with positioning							

6. Channel and location: Has determined the routes to market in line with ideal customer expectations				
7. Customer engagement: Has PR and marketing plan, social engagement strategy and processes for customer attraction, conversion and retention				
8. Supply chain: Knows where products will be sourced, what the supplier relationship management process is and has defined logistics processes				
9. Planning and controlling: Has documented plans for range, buying, costing, stock flow, cash flow and uses them to control and monitor the business				
10. Back office (HR, Legal, Fi and IT): Has determined organizational structure and resourcing plan, sourced appropriate professional services (Legal, Finance) and has a clear IT roadmap in place				

Step One
Goal and mission

Introduction

This chapter is Step 1 of the 10 steps retail success process. Arguably many of the elements in this step are not unique to retail businesses; they would be equally important to any type of business. I have, however, used retail examples to illustrate key points. Do take your time to really think about this chapter: it sets the focus for your action plan. You'll find that as we move on to the next steps it will be a great deal easier if you've been absolutely clear about your goal and mission as a result of this first step.

In this chapter we'll first take a look at your goals, both personal and business. Achieving a personal goal is often the fundamental reason why you are in business; working towards it will be what motivates you. Your business goal could be linked to how the business could enable you to realize your personal goal, or it might be independent of your personal goal. Either is fine; the main point is that your personal goals and business goals will not be the same.

Your personal goal is effectively about defining your 'life strategy' – not an area we'll spend much time on; if you want to delve deeper into that then I recommend you take a look at a specific text on the topic; there are many. In the same way that your personal goal is your life strategy you could consider your business goal(s) to be synonymous with your business strategy, and in order to achieve your business goals/strategy you need to break them down into an action plan. **The focus of this book in its entirety is to support you in drawing together each of the strategic and operational strands of a retail business in order to translate your current business goals into a set of executable actions.** These will form the basis of your business action plan that will enable you to progress from where you are today to where you want to be.

In the second part of this chapter we'll look at the importance of your values and beliefs. We'll consider how these influence the actions that you will choose to take, as a business owner, to achieve your business and personal goals.

Finally we'll look at how you can encapsulate the business purpose into a compelling mission statement that can be used to communicate the guiding principles of your business to others – suppliers, customers, staff:

anyone. We'll work through an example to demonstrate the value of having a clear mission statement to refer back to when you are faced with making a tough decision about the direction your business should take.

At the end of this chapter I hope that you will have taken some time to reflect on the differences and similarities between your personal and business goals. Document these somewhere so you can refer back to them if you ever need to remind yourself why you are in business. You don't need to make them public or share them with anyone if you don't want to; it's just that sometimes it helps to have a statement of your goals to reflect on, to boost your confidence when things get tough, as they always do from time to time. Also by the end of this chapter you'll have set down your 'boundaries' – those values and beliefs that are so important to you that they will affect what you consider to be acceptable, or not, in your business. Finally you'll have created that compelling mission statement – and if you've got it right you'll be excited about sharing it with others.

So, let's first take a closer look at your personal goal.

Defining your personal goal

Although this isn't a book on personal or life coaching I've found it to be absolutely essential when working with clients for the first time to begin the 10 steps to retail success process with a conversation about their personal goal.

A business owner with a business but no personal goal is like someone with a map but no idea where they are going. Your personal goal is all about your deep-rooted ambitions, dreams, wishes and feelings that motivate you, that keep you on track and when the going gets tough, that stop you from giving up. Consider your personal goal to be like the destination for your journey; while you absolutely should enjoy 'getting there' at the end of the day you wouldn't embark on a journey if you didn't know where you were going; you start out with the end, the destination, in mind. The same has to be true with your business – although you might not have thought of it like that before!

As a business owner never underestimate the influence your personal goal will have on the way you go about running your business. It will be an influencing factor to all those decisions you appear to make on 'gut feel'. When it's clear in your mind you will realize that your personal goal runs a thread through all that you do.

Reflect on this; ask yourself some questions, which might include:

- What is my personal goal?
- How does that connect to my retail business?
- What made me decide to embark on this journey?
- What is my destination and how will I know when I've arrived there?

Write down the answers to these questions, and anything else you feel is relevant that comes to mind. Keep your notes to refer back to. These thoughts will be important and unique to you. They will help you to understand how to navigate your way through the difficult decisions that you will inevitably be faced with on your business journey. Of course with the twists and turns that life throws at you, you may find that you no longer want to aim for the same goal. If so you need to think about changing your destination, re-routing your business, and then proceeding with your journey to achieve your new aims.

When I first met Sarah Decent, owner of Modish, the shoe shop business, we established that her personal goal was:

> **Sarah's Goal:** 'I want to sell the business in five years for a million pounds. This will be my retirement nest egg.'

In this statement the personal goal is 'to create a retirement nest egg of £1 million'.

Another retailer I know has quite a different goal in mind. Anna is an attractive woman in her late thirties. She suffered with breast cancer and had a double mastectomy. Now she is fully recovered, and her experiences have changed her life, as you might expect! One of her frustrations was that having recovered from such a horrific illness she found that there was nowhere to buy beautiful lingerie, swimwear and evening wear for her post-operative figure. She wanted to get back to 'normal life' as much as possible and not give up wearing the kind of clothes she loved. As a result of uncovering this gap in the market she is developing a range of garments for women just like her.

> **Anna's Goal:** 'To draw a fair salary for myself and to put all profits from the business into breast cancer charities.'

In this statement the personal goal is 'to create an ongoing revenue for breast cancer charities; to give something back'.

Another example of a goal is to create a family business that will be a source of income for your family, and for their family, etc.

With each unique person comes a unique personal goal. This isn't typically something you'd share openly with your staff or your friends, perhaps it's something you only tell your partner, or perhaps you would prefer to keep it to yourself. Whatever your goal is, just remember the influence it will have over you, your motivation and the way you create and operate your business. It's important that you take some time to identify what your personal goal is. It will have an impact on your business goal; which we'll explore in more detail now.

Your business goal

Although inevitably connected to your personal goal, your business goal is – rather stating the obvious – a lot less personal! Business goals are all about measurable achievements – rate of growth, number of employees, number of stores, amount of turnover, increased profitability, dividend pay-out, valuation, etc.

As a business owner it is likely that your business goal(s) will be the set of achievements that the business makes (under your leadership) that mean you attain your personal goal.

Let me illustrate this with an example. Earlier I shared with you Sarah's personal goal – to create a retirement nest egg of £1 million. She had gone some way to joining the personal and business goals as she had mindfully chosen to buy a business with the intent to sell it at a future date – ideally five years forward – in order to realize her personal goal. However, when I met Sarah she was about two years down the line and felt very 'lost' – her personal goal was clear, a beacon and guiding light, keeping her on track and focused, *but* in the absence of how to translate that personal goal into her business goal she was frustrated – she knew her business needed a boost, was not 'optimized' and, her biggest fear, she did not actually know what to do to turn it into a business that would realize that sale value of £1 million.

I recall having the first 1-2-1 with Sarah, before she became my first 'retail champion mentoring programme' client. Sarah explained her reasons for buying her business and her personal goal. To me the way forward was clear. Together we needed to find a way that was comfortable for Sarah to connect her personal goal to the business.

To realize her target sales value of £1 million there is a variety of formulae one can use. Different kinds of businesses – eg technology development vs consumer facing – have very different models for valuation. I'd done a bit of research and we agreed that for a traditional retail model, with purely scalability of operation on its side in terms of increased growth/profit potential, we should probably err on the side of caution when considering how her business would ultimately be valued. We agreed what her annual profit should be when she put the business up for sale, based on the current market, in order to get her asking price of £1 million.

Here on in, it was relatively easy to carve out the business goal(s) – we knew the annual profitability of the two shops she currently retailed from, we knew the performance of her website, thus we determined that should she expand to a chain of eight to 10 stores with a more productive website, even though there would be additional overheads of storage/distribution and some level of 'head office' infrastructure, she would (assuming all stores delivered the same average profitability of those she already had) realize the level of total profitability that would attract a buyer willing to pay £1 million.

So that was the business goal – to grow to be a chain of 10 stores, with a strong transactional website in five years' time in order to then realize a sales value of £1 million. Sorted!

Of course below that bold statement was a massive amount of work – together we needed to develop a robust, repeatable set of processes and systems to enable Sarah to present a scalable, saleable business to market;

but now we had our target. From here we could break that down into a plan that would look far more realistic and achievable than perhaps at first glance. I am sure if someone boldly stated to you 'you need to open eight new retail outlets, revamp your e-commerce presence and set up a head office, all within five years' you might think they were mad, but it's not that crazy. In fact, many retail entrepreneurs have achieved a great deal more, and a great deal more quickly. They are proof that it can be done!

As mentioned before, each business owner achieves their goals in very different ways: each unique, personal and underpinned by their values and beliefs, which we'll explore in more detail now.

Values and beliefs

The late Anita Roddick, founder of The Body Shop, had a goal and a passion. **She wanted to change the world.** That was her goal. I'd like to share a story that I was told by Nigel Rothband, currently chief executive of the charity Retail Trust. He used to be on the board of directors for The Body Shop when Anita was still at the helm.

Nigel once challenged Anita in a board meeting about a decision that she supported. He asserted to her that this decision would be less profitable than an alternative option. She shot him down, quite fiercely, defending her absolute belief that she was not in business for profit, she was in business to change the world! You can imagine that this came as a bit of a surprise, but Nigel told me it was also very moving, and something that has stayed with him ever since.

The moral of the story is that **when you, as the business owner, have a goal that you will defend so passionately you need to recognize that others may not necessarily understand that** (not to begin with). Their previous experience of employment may have taught them a different set of behaviours from those you want to instil in your business. Bear that in mind – because what is obvious and ingrained to you may be alien and confusing to those around you. As an outsider looking in, one would be forgiven for making the assumption that Anita wanted to produce and sell natural, ethical, sustainable health and beauty products. Indeed she did, but her personal goal was so much deeper than that.

That brief insight into how Anita Roddick ran The Body Shop, which I learned from someone who worked closely with her in her lifetime, demonstrates why it is not only your goal but also your values and beliefs that permeate your entire business. Your values and beliefs will influence how it will be structured; how it should be run. In Anita's case her personality – goal, values and beliefs – became the culture; and for those working at The Body Shop, this was a given. Anita's value system attracted suppliers, staff and a whole customer base who shared her beliefs (and equally deterred those who did not). After she was diagnosed with cancer she sold the business to L'Oréal. A number of the senior management left the business at that time. Perhaps they felt that without Anita as the figurehead, and the conscience of the business, it would no longer provide them with the culture that they were so wholly bought into. To the consumer it appears that L'Oréal continue to operate The Body Shop based on the core values and beliefs that Anita supported – a significant challenge for a global megabrand – but they really have no choice. If they didn't remain committed to the core values they'd soon see the customers, who became loyal to The Body Shop because of what Anita stood for, drifting away and seeking other alternatives.

Long after a business owner sells a business that has a culture and value set that are unique to them the business can retain the essence of what the owner stood for. Anita Roddick's brand The Body Shop is evidence of this.

So, let's take a look at what's important to you.

When working 1-2-1 with clients I always ask them to spend some time considering what means most to them. You should do this exercise. Answer these questions and keep hold of the answers:

- What are your values and beliefs?
- How will they shape your business?
- What ethical areas are a no-go – where are your boundaries?
- What do you want your business to 'stand for' – does it have a 'message'?

Let me give you some examples. They're not all relevant to all businesses but just indicative of the kind of questions you might ask yourself to define your boundaries.

Would you ever sell cigarettes?

Some business owners, even those with a convenience retail offering, may *never* be willing to sell cigarettes. Their belief may be that they don't want to encourage smoking; and this may be based on a personal experience of a family member affected by smoking-related diseases.

Although it may not be a profitable decision it will surely be one that as the business owner, if ever challenged by your staff on the topic, you will defend passionately.

Would you restrict your offer to retailing only locally produced merchandise?

You may want to do so for environmental reasons, you may want to reduce the impact of an extended supply chain. You may have economic reasons for your decisions – believing that by supporting other local businesses (producers, makers) you are adding value back to your community. It may be purely commercial – you can stand out from the crowd and attract consumers who are willing to pay a premium for local products.

Whatever your reasons, the outcome will be a clearly defined boundary. If you were ever presented with a product that could really increase your profitability that was *not* locally produced, you'd reject it. Business advisors may think you are mad, *but* – and this is critical to remember – as the owner of a smaller business (with plans to grow) **you must be true to your values and beliefs or you will risk becoming disenchanted with your business; eroding your passion, motivation and ultimately your ability to achieve your goal.**

Whatever your beliefs are they will mean a lot to you and will stamp a mark on your business. What you stand for will be attractive for some customers, but not for others. As these are *your* beliefs, you have to recognize that and be happy with it. If you can't reconcile your values and beliefs with a business model that will realize your personal goal then maybe you need to reconsider what you are trying to do.

The next step is to define the mission for your business. Now we've confirmed the goal, and the values and beliefs that will shape your business, we're going to be focusing on the real fundamentals of what your business is all about.

Defining the mission

Defining your mission statement is a very straightforward process and very powerful. It will take a couple of attempts to get it right – but when you do you will *know* it is right and you will feel proud to share it with staff, suppliers and customers. **A mission statement will tell anyone, in about 50 words, exactly what your business does.**

The other benefit of a mission statement is that whenever you are faced with a difficult decision in the business, you can choose the path you need to take by asking yourself the question: 'Does this deliver on my mission?'

While your mission is the key message that explains what your business is about to all those involved (employees, suppliers, customers) it should not constrain you. There may be times when you need to change your business model or focus due to economic influences, technology and trends. You can obviously change your mission statement accordingly. The point is that while it can evolve with your business that evolution should always be for the right reasons. If your mission is the key message that those involved in your business have bought into, once communicated, you can't keep changing it.

First of all let's look at what a mission statement actually is. Typically a mission statement should be about 50 to 60 words. It should include four key statements:

1 What you offer – in as simple and understandable terms as possible, you should explain what your business sells (products and services).

2 Who you offer it to – again, as clearly as possible, who you (ideally) sell to – the generic description of your customer.

3 Your service proposition – this is about explaining what the customer experience is like, how you deliver your offer to the customer and what is or is not included in the process.

4 The outcome for your customer – finally, this is how your customer should benefit from buying from you; how they feel as a result or quite literally what the experience of buying from you achieves for them as an outcome.

Example mission statements

In order to bring this concept to life I'm going to share the mission statements for two very different areas of my businesses, The Retail Champion and Albans Office Space.

Let's start with The Retail Champion as my first example:
The Retail Champion offers retail expertise and bespoke business mentoring programmes to business owners who are either retailers or suppliers to retail. Retailers will develop robust and repeatable processes and systems; suppliers to retail will create a compelling value proposition and go to market strategy. Thus, The Retail Champion enables *all* clients to become scalable, saleable businesses.
(57 words)

I personally find that it's easiest both to create a mission statement and to work through it by breaking it down into the constituent parts. So, looking again at the statement for The Retail Champion this is how it is comprised:

1 The proposition – what you offer: 'The Retail Champion offers retail expertise and bespoke business mentoring programmes'.

2 The target market – who you offer it to: 'to business owners who are either retailers or suppliers to retail'.

3 The delivery – your service proposition: 'Retailers will develop robust and repeatable processes and systems; suppliers to retail will create a compelling value proposition and go to market strategy.'

4 The outcome for your customer: 'Thus, The Retail Champion enables *all* clients to become scalable, saleable businesses.'

It probably isn't perfect but it says enough about what I offer, to whom, how I deliver, and what my customers' experiences are as a result.

I've found it very useful to use this mission statement on several occasions – it has really helped me to deliver a succinct 'elevator pitch' when asked the dreaded question at a networking event 'What do you do?'. As my business is made up of several different brands it's also been a really effective way to communicate more about what I offer through The Retail Champion brand when we have brought new staff into the business.

Think about your business; if you had a mission statement would you find it easier to explain what your business is all about to your staff? Could you use each of the four elements to remind them, as part of a team, what they are expected to deliver? Could you use each element, expanded, to really give them an overview of your business and your vision? I've personally found that my staff engagement levels increase when I talk staff through the mission statement; if I take time to explain it, to break it down, and stick to the basic four elements. I can see that they 'get' the brand and as a result their passion for the brand, and loyalty to the business, increases.

My second example is Albans Office Space:

I also own another business, completely separate to my retail-centric brands. This is a serviced and virtual office business based in St Albans rather appropriately called 'Albans Office Space'. This is a very different proposition from The Retail Champion. I'm going to share the mission statement for Albans Office Space as it will help to illustrate that irrespective of what you offer or who you offer it to, your mission statement is very powerful. It will not be a waste of your time to spend 30 minutes or so working it out.

As it happens I'm not generally active in the day-to-day running of the serviced offices business so, for me, as one of the owning directors, I find the mission statement a really great reminder of what we're about and who we are for. It helps me to arbitrate in any tough decision making – I can ask the team 'In what way does following this course of action meet our mission?'; if they can demonstrate that they've understood how a proposed action does support our mission I'm usually comfortable to sign it off. Equally, if they cannot demonstrate that crucial aspect to the decision-making process then I would usually ask the team to reconsider.

Our mission statement enables us to take away personal perspectives from what otherwise could become more heated business discussions. It helps to remove the risk of employees stating 'Well, the directors just didn't want to do what I proposed' – this kind of arbitration through the mission statement will be incredibly valuable to you in your business, especially as you begin to outgrow the detailed level of management and need to employ managers for your stores to take delegated decisions for you.

Anyway, this is what Albans Office Space is all about:

Albans Office Space offers professional workspace, meeting facilities, and virtual office services to business people who want to meet at, work in or grow their business from our St Albans location. We are friendly, welcoming and supportive of customer needs so customers feel that their business is as important to us as our own.

(54 words)

1 The proposition – what you offer: 'Albans Office Space offers professional workspace, meeting facilities, and virtual office services'.

2 The target market – who you offer it to: 'to business people who want to meet at, work in or grow their business from our St Albans location'.

3 The delivery – your service proposition: 'We are friendly, welcoming and supportive of customer needs'.

4 The outcome for your customer: 'so customers feel that their business is as important to us as our own'.

As you can probably see from the above, the mission really helps 'ground' the business and encapsulates all that it stands for in a way that is readily understandable to anyone else. It very clearly states who the service is ideally offered for and what it feels like to be a customer.

Using your mission statement as a decision support tool

I'd like to reflect back on the point I raised above regarding the times I've asked staff to reflect on how their proposed decisions do (or do not) fit in with our mission statement. I'd like to show you, with a real-life example, how you can use your mission statement to help you make difficult decisions for your business. While I'm not at liberty to disclose the name of the retailer in question I can assure you the story that follows is true and that the consultant in question is a well-known business advisor.

Example 1 – Independent furniture retailer

In 2010 an independent furniture retailer in southwest London engaged a well-known and well-regarded retail consultant to revamp their business. The process involved a great deal of change to their interior look and feel as well as to their product range and service proposition. Until the point when the changes were implemented their marketing and product offer had been aligned, their customers knew them for what they sold, and they did a reasonable trade. They wanted to improve their performance and become more effective, hence why they engaged outside support.

As a result of the changes their customers were surprised to discover that neither the store interior nor the product range matched their expectations – so they stopped purchasing. The marketing materials reflected the old proposition – so people who were attracted to the proposition based on the marketing were sorely disappointed when what they were presented with in store was not what they expected. The retailer had repositioned their business but with no communication to the market they were letting down past and potential customers left, right and centre. It was a mess and they were really in difficulties.

I found out about this retailer when I read a post on a social media forum – it was from one of the team who had been working on the project asking members of the forum if they had any ideas about how to save this retailer!

Luckily, this retailer didn't need saving; they survived. They reverted back to much of their old positioning, restoring their identity and offer to what their loyal customers loved, and what the customers who had been attracted to the marketing materials expected.

While this example is about a retailer moving away from their marketed position, had the business owner had a mission statement to reflect on then perhaps they'd have thought about the proposed changes in the context of the four elements of the mission statement:

1 what you offer;

2 who you offer it to;

3 your service proposition;

4 the outcome for your customer.

With this in mind perhaps alarm bells would have been ringing when the proposed changes impacted on both elements one and three.

When considering business change you need a mission statement. It's as simple as that – if you don't have one you may make decisions that look great on paper but in reality could alienate your customers. I can't think of a single business that can survive for very long without customers!

Example 2 – Make-to-order curtain retailer

I have a second example; it is actually a story from my past. As I explained in the introduction I've grown up in a family of retailers. My grandparents ran a Nottinghamshire-based make-to-order curtain business, an offshoot from my parents' business. They made the product to order so that it was tailored to the customers' unique requirements. Customers paid in full at the time of order. Typically orders were made and despatched within a couple of weeks. In addition their business offered a free measurement and fitting service within the local area. This service was a strategy to reduce customer returns as the majority of these could be traced back to the customer not accurately measuring up or not knowing how to hang their new curtains. They had built up a good reputation that had enabled them to win contracts to supply orders taken through other local retailers as well. The business was reasonably profitable; my grandparents were better off than when they had been employed and they also provided employment for some 20 people. They were still keen to earn more; to be able to retire very comfortably and leave a nest egg for the family. So when an opportunity was presented for them to buy in stock of ready-made items at a very favourable price it seemed a great idea. There was no labour cost necessary; the factory team could continue to service the make-to-order sales. The items were priced such that their business would make a good margin on the sales even if the price point was lower than the lowest of all of the make-to-order options. It all looked viable and a not-to-be-missed opportunity on paper. BUT they had not considered two things:

1 Buying this product ahead of securing a customer for it was going to really hit their cash flow. Their cash-flow model was entirely based on a make-to-order mission. The uncut rolls of fabric were cheap to source and were only made up into curtains when a customer had placed an order and paid in full. Now they had bought into ready-made stock; although a favourable price it was still more expensive than unmade fabric. In those days the factory team could be laid off or asked to work extra hours at the drop of a hat, so the business really had no fixed costs beyond the raw materials. Suddenly they were faced with the issue of having higher-value stock and no guarantee of sales.

2 The ready-made curtains could be retailed more cheaply than the make-to-order product. This affected their order book as people chose the convenience and lower-cost option of buying ready-made items. Instead of an occasional short day on Fridays due to lower order volumes the factory team were working reduced hours on several days. Some were unable to sustain their own personal financial commitments and sought work elsewhere – so my grandparents lost loyal, skilled staff.

It was a bit of a mess, and it could have ruined their business. With cash flow tied up in stock, with resources unable to sustain reduced hours, they had to sell through that stock as quickly as possible. They needed to get the cash back into the business, remove the lower price point that encouraged customers to trade down, and boost the order book for make-to-order items so they could increase the working hours for factory staff again.

They made it through although it took several months. Had they have had a mission statement in place they could have considered that:

1 Their offer was make-to-order curtains, NOT ready made.

2 Their customer was a discerning individual who wanted something made to their taste, NOT a customer who was driven by convenience and who would make do with ready-made items.

3 Their customer experience should have been a bespoke service that included measuring and fitting so the customer could be sure that their new curtains would be perfect, NOT based on take some curtains away today and hope for the best!

4 The outcome should have been a customer who proudly shows off their new curtains to all their visitors and is evangelical about the wonderful service, NOT a customer who just about manages to put the ready-made, ill fitting, *cheap* curtains up at their window!

My example is probably a bit extreme; but I really wanted to get the point across – hopefully it worked. In this example the potential of the margin opportunity could have ruined my grandparents' business!

These two examples should reinforce for you how relevant a mission statement can be. So, before we move on to Step 2 I'd like you to use the mission statement structure I've provided and spend some time to create yours.

Summing up

Well done! You've completed Step 1 of the 10 steps to retail success. In this chapter we have looked at your goals, both personal and business. We considered how **your personal goals drive and motivate you** and I've asked you to spend some time to consider your personal goal and make a note of it somewhere.

We then looked at how this relates to your business goal. You should have also spent some time considering your business goal(s) for the next 1, 3, 5, 7, 10 years – whatever is meaningful to you. Make sure that you have documented them too; **your business goals will form the basis of your business plan, and will be a key influencer of everything you do.**

In the second part of this chapter we spent time considering the importance of your values and beliefs. We've looked at how these influence your business operations and how **your values and beliefs become your business culture.** We reflected on the way that your values and beliefs help you to define the boundaries for the way in which you are willing to achieve your goals, focusing on what you do want to stand for and what the real 'no-go areas' are for you. Ideally you'll have done some soul searching on this topic. It may seem intangible and unimportant now but when faced with a decision that feels 'uncomfortable' to you, if you can reference your 'business values, ethics and culture' as a set of statements, you may find the answer is there. This will be a reassuring document that means making tough decisions is much easier to do.

Finally we covered the **importance of capturing your business purpose into a compelling mission statement.** Having broken this down into its component parts, we've worked through how you can develop a mission statement that really captures the essence of what *your* business is all about.

As a result of completing this chapter you will now have a very clear basis for driving your business forward. Now it's time to move on to Step 2.

Step Two
Positioning

Introduction

Step 2 is all about positioning. In this chapter we're going to work through how to go about defining your positioning in terms of the four elements of which it is comprised: product, price, presentation and service. Each of these areas will be illustrated with examples and I'll ask you to honestly look at your business positioning.

We'll work through why many smaller businesses fall into the trap of trying to be all things to all people, and in this chapter I am going to introduce one of my strongest points: that your positioning is fundamental to your customer service delivery. **Positioning is how your brand/business makes 'promises' to your customers, either explicit or implied, and as a result of those promises you have the ability to disappoint or to delight your customers!**

I'll also be talking about competition, and **another trap smaller businesses fall into, underpricing and over-serving.**

At the end of this chapter you will have considered your current positioning and identified any areas that need 'alignment' to enable you to be more profitable, more sustainable. We'll have considered the impact of how your brand positioning influences your attractiveness to customers, and how being out of kilter only serves to confuse. Finally we'll ensure that having worked through this chapter you can confidently be positioned so that you **don't compete on price, you compete on service!**

So, what *is* positioning?

In the last chapter when you created your mission statement you made a confident, bold statement about your business. You have clearly communicated what you offer (the product or service), who you offer it to (the ideal customer group), how you go about it (your service proposition) and the result (the outcome for your customer who has bought from you).

That's great – but it is just a starting point. Now we need to take a look at what *positioning* is all about, how it is relevant to your business, and how you can use it to give you confidence in your decisions.

Positioning is based on an assessment of where you 'sit' relative to your competition with regard to four key areas – product, price, presentation and service. In this day and age your competition could be a group so vast and diverse that it would be almost impossible to attempt to place yourself in a comparison with them all. So, as part of your positioning exercise I'd like you to spend a moment to consider this question: What are the most likely alternatives that your ideal customer group might consider when planning to purchase what YOU offer?

Let me illustrate this with an example. If your mission statement states that your business offers chauffeur-driven cars for business people in and around Manchester then your competition would neither be mini cabs nor would it be 'party limousines' in Manchester. Your competition would also not be chauffeurs in Birmingham. You should consider that if your ideal customer is in need of a car and driver for business travel in and around Manchester then likely as not their PA would *only* research options within the relevant catchment area and would surely rule out those who were not sufficiently professional for the executive who had requested the booking be made. In this way you can be more specific about who your competition is, and you can consider how you are positioned in comparison to the most relevant competitive set more easily.

To illustrate this concept of positioning relative to your competitive set I'm going to walk you through an example based on something you will hopefully be familiar with – airlines. Even if you've not flown with any of those I've mentioned in the example, because of how well these brands market their positioning, you probably will have a good idea of what they are all about.

So let's look at a competitive set made up of:

- easyJet;
- British Airways;
- Ryanair;
- Virgin Atlantic.

Let's assume all four of these airlines offer a route that a customer wants and a timetable that's acceptable to them. Those criteria, the ability to offer broadly what the customer wants, when they want it, rule all four of these airlines into our 'competitive set' because the consumer of their services will potentially consider them side by side; price compare them, look at all the other add-ons they include, their reputation, etc. Perhaps our customer has already ruled out Emirates, Qantas and Lufthansa – possibly because they don't offer the basic route or timetable needed.

I hope already you can see why my point about a realistic and relevant competitive set is key to this activity – a consumer never considers the 'whole of market' perspective, they consider the market relevant (and known) to them. Yes, they are likely to research their options online; but they'll still only look at a reduced group in greater detail. That's why I've illustrated this point with just four airlines when in reality there are many more if you consider the total market view.

Moving forward with this example, as I've already explained, the four shortlisted providers can broadly meet the consumer's needs. We cannot second-guess every customer's motivations for choosing a provider; however, the mission statement can specify which type of customer we're going to target as a business. Remember '**business** cars in Manchester' – we ruled in customers whose decision factor was work travel and ruled out those who wanted a car for leisure. I'm sure the chauffeuring business could have serviced the requirements of a leisure customer, but the mission, and thus the positioning, was focused on business customers.

The same is true for our airlines. We know they do compete for the same people as customers. They may even share customers; for example, an individual might buy from easyJet for personal travel and from Virgin for business. The final choice depends on our consumer's reason for the journey (business vs leisure), how convenient the option is (the detail of the flight timetables) and what 'opinion' our customer has regarding the 'suitability' of the airline in terms of meeting their expectations. This 'suitability' will be something the airlines have led the customer to believe as a result of their positioning.

Let's assume then that this is a leisure flight. Without too much research you may already have an opinion about which airline you'd most want to travel with, and why. Some customers might be more than happy with Ryanair or easyJet at the lower end – they just want the most cost-effective trip to keep as much of their budget for the experiences once they arrive. Other people may never even consider the budget airlines; they would want British Airways or Virgin Atlantic at the upper end. To them the higher cost is money well spent on a comfortable journey – all part of their leisure experience.

OK – this seems pretty obvious but my questions are:

- How did the customer know which airline they would prefer?
- Without prior experience of all four on the route in question, what did they base their opinions on?

The answer is positioning. From their branding to their marketing materials, everything that's 'communicated' to the customer creates that 'opinion' regarding what it would be like to be a customer of the brand. The words, images and all outward representations of the brand create an impression. While feedback from past customers regarding their experiences with a brand do reinforce the assumptions we form about that brand, **the four elements of positioning – product, price, presentation and service – all work together in harmony to attract (or repel) those customers we're planning to attract (or repel).** Let's look at how.

Breaking down the four elements of positioning

It is commonly accepted that positioning includes four elements, although you may hear them described differently. I have used the terminology 'product, price, presentation and service' although I've read various other ways of expressing the same thing. Terminology is not critical – it's what it means that matters.

Product: what the customer gets

This includes the features and benefits, the 'bells and whistles', the ingredients. It generically covers physical goods as well as services.

In the airline example above the product was a flight from A to B. In terms of positioning, all of the 'other stuff' (higher hold-baggage allowances, plusher interior, in-flight meal, attentive cabin crew, optional access to departure lounges, business and first-class upgrades, etc) that you get – generally speaking – included in the price (or upgrade option) on a Virgin or BA flight are the 'ingredients' that lead us to understand it is a 'higher-end' offer. Compare that to easyJet or Ryanair, where at one time (I am sure you recall) it was suggested that even using the toilets in-flight would be an additional charge! Certainly everything about the product is stripped back to the very bare minimum, the essentials. These are called 'no-frills' airlines for good reason – but if you only want to travel, by air, from place A to place B, then that is enough. At the end of the day customers only accept the product if the next element, pricing, seems fair. Together the product and price represent value to the customer.

Pricing: what you are asked to pay for the product

In the airline example, because of the different ingredients included with the product, you will expect to pay more for the BA or Virgin flight. That could be because you recognize the value of the 'extras'.

If BA or Virgin ran a promotion that brought their pricing closer to easyJet or Ryanair then potentially consumers who were most keen on price, or those with limited budget, would feel comfortable trading up. This is a risk and blurs the lines on price positioning. When higher-end brands start to compete on price, attracting a more price-sensitive customer, their regular customer base may become disillusioned. The regular customer perhaps enjoyed a certain sense of exclusivity that paying a premium price point afforded them. Now, with a more accessible price point, the brand risks alienating high-spending, non-price-sensitive customers because they no longer feel they're in an exclusive group.

Smaller retail businesses need to be very aware of this as they often feel that they should cave in to the enormous price pressure that comes from the major supermarkets and online mega-retailers like Amazon. The risk is that when you reduce the price you attract a more price-sensitive audience. A lady I know who runs a marketing agency warns about 'HELP' customers – these are typically struggling, purely after a deal, and to whom price is paramount. HELP describes these customers – they have HIGH EXPECTATIONS but are LOW PROFITABILITY for your business. Remember that!

Generally speaking easyJet and Ryanair are providing services to the lower end of the market and Virgin and BA provide services to the middle and higher end. If higher-end pricing gets too close to low end then they attract a customer who may trade up, perhaps overstretch themselves a little, and then they will expect the earth for it! This is quite common and is the primary reason I urge smaller retail businesses to reflect on how they can use pricing to really influence who their customer is. Less is often more in that fewer, higher-spending customers, comfortable with parting with their money, are easier to service than many low-spending customers who struggle to spend with ease, or at all.

So, back to the elements of positioning: we've covered product and price, next comes presentation. Where product and price are explicit 'promises' that your brand makes which lead to customer expectations, presentation is very much about the implied promise.

Presentation: the outward representation to the world of that brand

Logo, colours, shop front, advertising, website, packaging… Everything that the public can see of your brand right down to the uniform that the staff wear. This all gives an impression, a 'feeling' for what being a customer of the brand will be like. This is an area where brands can go horribly wrong as the outward representation makes implied promises to customers.

In the airline example you don't even need to read too much about the product – you can see immediately that the 'polish' (well-presented staff, glossy marketing materials, rich 'quality' colours, attention to detail in all of their outward branding) is evident with BA and Virgin. However, in keeping with the sense of 'no frills', Ryanair and easyJet look a bit cheaper. Although staff are still uniformed and aircraft are all consistently branded, the whole 'look' is somehow consistent with the product and price – it's just not as 'glossy'; even the websites – take a look – they're just not quite as luxurious as the other two. Functional? Yes. Elegant? No.

This area is such a minefield to the smaller business. In the most part before someone purchases from you they will have noticed your brand. In fact in 2011 it was quoted that over 60 per cent of consumers have researched online before making an in-store purchase. Google claim that over 90 per cent of *all* purchases will be influenced by material online before 2020. So, working with a design agency who you have a great rapport with, who you trust, who have experience in your sector, and who have evidence of working with other successful businesses on similar projects, will be key to getting this part just right.

A good agency will really understand your mission, positioning, values and business goals. They will work with you to develop a visual identity for your brand that is far wider reaching that just a logo, business card and website design – it's about colours, fonts, styles, themes as well. You should invest wisely with designers and with your brand presentation. Think long and hard about where your ideal customers are likely to 'happen across you' and ensure that the materials published about you deliver the impression you want – this is the presentation element of your positioning. At the end of this chapter I'll use an example of why presentation can make a fairly ordinary product (tea and cake) worth an incredible price! Presentation makes your customer feel that they are getting something of exceptional value, or not. I'll also share an example of an independent fashion boutique, Amabo who are based in Lytham St Annes. Natalie Peters, the owner of Amabo, makes sure her presentation is exceptional regardless of the amount a customer spends on each visit. In this way she is linking presentation ultimately to the customer service experience and that leads us on to the final element of positioning – service delivery.

Service: the way you are treated as a customer

It's all the value-added extras you get when you buy a product. It's to do with the whole purchasing experience as well the after-sales service, handling of issues, returns policy and guarantees.

Finally, and perhaps the most important element in terms of the customer experience, is service. Service proves that all the assumptions made thus far about the quality of a brand – from the product, price and presentation – are borne out. This is where your business has to live up to all the implied and explicit promises you've made through the previous three elements.

If you think John Lewis you think exceptional customer service delivery. Argos is another interesting one. The price positioning requires a much less elaborate in-store experience; however, Argos does offer a very solid total service delivery. Although not 'high end' like John Lewis, I would position Argos at the top of their competitive set with excellent options for home delivery, store collection and a very good returns policy. Argos stands out from its competition – which used to include Woolworths and now mainly includes supermarkets as well as retailers like ToysRus, Wilkinson and Robert Dyas. John Lewis has to stand out against a much more high-end offering – they are in a competitive set with House of Fraser, Debenhams and even Selfridges, Harvey Nichols and Harrods. However, and possibly due to their partnership model, they have some of the most helpful, well trained and long-serving staff, meaning they consistently deliver outstanding service, completing their extremely well executed positioning!

It's not just about one element; it's about all four in alignment

There is more to positioning than just the four elements – no one of the elements alone makes your positioning – it's the relationships between all four elements of positioning that really count. For a business to present a congruent and profitable offering, all four elements of positioning need to be in alignment (when compared to the competitive set).

Let's review easyJet in the context of alignment in its positioning:

- **The product**: no frills, it's just a seat on an aircraft going from A to B.
- **The price**: it's stripped back, and congruent in terms with the product quality.
- **Presentation**: it's 'what you see is what you get'. They've used brand colours that are considered to evoke a 'cheaper' emotion – the orange and white are brash, not luxurious.
- **Service**: It's minimal. You pay for anything extra. There's no added value. Again, this is congruent with everything they've led us to expect with product, price and presentation.

Result? They are successful. There are no nasty surprises for the customer because you've not been led to believe you're getting anything beyond transport in the first place.

Visually you could use a model I find very useful when giving talks about positioning – I call it 'the arrows'; you may have come across it before.

Compared to the easyJet competitive set you could say they are more 'downmarket' or 'positioned lower' – so visually when each element of the positioning is at the lower end of the range for the competitive set you could imagine an arrow pointing downwards.

When all the arrows point in the same direction then all four elements of positioning are aligned. If just one of these steps is out of synch, if the arrows point in different directions, then the implications could be crippling for their business. WHY? Because through their positioning they are making both implied and explicit promises to the customer about what their whole experience will be. If they fail on any of those promises *or* if they over-deliver they'll either have set an expectation with their customers which they fail to deliver on, leading to disappointment *or* they'll have undervalued their offering, falling into the same trap that many smaller businesses fall into, of underpricing and over-serving.

TABLE 2.1   Using 'the arrows' method to determine how you are positioned relative to the competitive set

	Product	Price	Presentation	Service
easyJet	⬇	⬇	⬇	⬇
Ryanair	⬇	⬇	⬇	⬇
Virgin	⬆	⬆	⬆	⬆
BA	⬆	⬆	⬆	⬆

Think about it: if you sell a cheap product for a high price customers will become disillusioned, if they buy at all. If you sell a quality product for a low price you'll make too little profit to survive. If you sell a quality product and deliver excellent service, charge a high price but look cheap you'll simply not attract customers willing to pay your prices; if you sell a cheap product and offer basic service but look luxurious, once again you'll attract the wrong kind of customer – they'll expect more from you than you've got to offer.

Can you see how it would work for your business? Ask yourself: What 'mistakes' am I making when it comes to my positioning?

You might be able to get some quick wins in terms of attracting the right customers or making more profit if you look at the alignment of your arrows. I am sure lots of smaller retailers reading this book recognize that they have an arrow out of alignment. I'd hazard a guess that the arrow not in synch with the others is the 'price'. It won't be for everyone, but the most significant number of smaller retailers I meet fall into the trap of trying to compete on price where that is not congruent with the three other elements of their positioning. Perhaps it's because you've seen John Lewis being 'never knowingly undersold' – but ask someone at the John Lewis Partnership what that means: it's about a price match not only on a comparable item but one with a comparable service proposition: warranty, returns policy, delivery options, the whole package. Suddenly their base price matches favourably with any competitor who may appear to be cheaper because no one else can compete on service. **Remember, when you can't compete on price, compete on service.**

How this affects your customer service experience

My mantra about why customers feel they have been given bad service links to positioning – because it is often through positioning that without even realizing it you are making promises to your customers, implied or explicit, about what the customer experience of your business will be... so I hope you will remember:

> When your brand makes promises, implied or explicit, these set expectations with your customer. If you fail to deliver on those promises you will fail to deliver the expected customer experience.

Before we move off this point I want to share one more example about an independent fashion boutique who intuitively knew how to protect their positioning, although at the time didn't quite realize why.

Amabo Boutique

Earlier I mentioned Amabo Boutique in Lytham St Annes, run by Natalie Peters. Without even realizing it Natalie was fiercely protecting Amabo's higher-end positioning. On a webinar Natalie asked me a question:

> Should I continue to give my customers my high-quality carrier bags and still tissue wrap their garments even when they are buying clearance items or items from the end-of-season sale? Other retailers in the area seem to use a cheaper 'sale' bag. Should I be doing the same?

I rapidly reassured Natalie that she was doing the right thing. Her positioning, a high-end ladies' fashion boutique, required that her total customer experience be a delightful and rewarding experience, regardless of transaction size. Her customers very much enjoyed shopping with Amabo, leaving the store with their purchases all beautifully wrapped and carefully placed in a luxurious-looking bag. No one would guess that the customer had been frugally buying from the sale rail – and because of that the customers very proudly carried out their purchases, for all to see, in an attractive bag covered in Amabo's branding. Natalie was ensuring that both her presentation and her service delivery were consistently delivered to her customer base at all times.

Had Natalie provided a lower level of service in the sale it might have saved her a little money but the impact on her customer experience, their ongoing loyally to her, their likelihood to recommend Amabo to friends, would have been at risk. Plus, with a non-branded 'sale' bag the Amabo branding would not have been noticed by passers-by. Using branded bags ensured Amabo got maximum exposure, perhaps catching the attention of other potential customers who might also want to visit this store with the 'posh bags'!

I think the Amabo example brings to life the subtleties that can make all the difference to your positioning.

Now I want to go back to a point I made earlier: **when you can't compete on price, compete on service.** I mentioned this above, and this is an area I really want to focus on with you in more detail in this chapter. I find myself repeating this point over and over again. In fact I've already said it a couple of times in this chapter!

If you can't compete on price (which as an independent I would suggest you can't) then compete on service. Think John Lewis...

As a rule it seems that some wonderful small businesses (and this is not exclusive to retailers by any means) seem to believe that to compete they should *over-serve* and *underprice*. The retailers in particular feel that, being small, and in the face of the sheer power of the multiples, they need to compete on both price and service. The two cannot work together. To put it in terms of positioning, the arrows are not aligned. Smaller retailers really can have the edge when it comes to service. They can get to know their customers so well that they can deliver an experience so aligned to what the customer wants that they'd certainly not choose to shop elsewhere if they could help it!

Reflect on the outcome of the exercise you did to consider your positioning in the context of your competitive set.

- Where were you placing yourself compared to the competition?
- Were all your arrows aligned and pointing in the same direction?
- Is your service arrow pointing upwards?
- What direction is your price arrow pointing?

Earlier I predicted it would be the price arrow that was out of alignment.

As a smaller business you really need to think about shifting your positioning towards the higher end: you can't compete on price with the retail giants. Why should you even try to compete on price with other retailers? In the end all that happens is that you create a price war – a downward spiral. In this situation the retailer with greatest buying power will win, and that's not you. That's because the big player's volumes give them considerable leverage in supplier negotiations. In the meantime you'll be eroding your own retail margins and those of the other retailers trying to compete with you. It simply isn't sustainable. Something will give and those with the least financial buffer will cave in.

Obviously there are products that consumers will know the price point to; so for these 'known value items' (KVIs) you will need to stay competitive. My advice, however, is to retail a more differentiated assortment – don't confuse your customer, but do try and sell items that:

1 they won't easily be able to find elsewhere; and

2 don't have a known/expected price point.

Don't forget that if you are located in a high street or neighbourhood location, and offer consumers a convenient and accessible option compared to driving to a supermarket, that also has a value. If all the consumer needs are a few things for dinner tonight then they're probably happy to pay a slightly premium price to avoid the extra time, effort and journey to an out-of-town location.

So use what you can to reinforce your value proposition to your customers. Your independent position enables you to offer products that consumers can't easily price compare. Likely as not, your location means you are a convenient alternative to a supermarket or shopping centre *and* if you offer a compelling service proposition then you are going to be able to raise prices quite justifiably. You will be offering a unique range of high-quality, high-price merchandise, with exceptional service and beautiful presentation – you've positioned with all your arrows upwards. If you happen to be situated in a more convenient location then that's an added bonus!

When you position your prices at the low end you need volume, lots and lots of volume, to make money. Look at Tesco over the years: as they increased in scale they were able to become aggressive on price. Until you've got that chain of shops, you really must think **service!**

However, even when you've got a chain of shops I would recommend you *still* think service. The reason I say this is because there are a number of factors changing the face of the retail market globally:

- increasing access to the internet, in part fuelled by mobile devices, that enables consumers to research prices, identify alternatives, and to share experiences, good or bad, on social networks and dedicated review websites;
- the shifting role of high street/community retail;
- the fall-out of the recent global economic downturn.

There is already evidence to suggest that consumer behaviour is creating polarization in the retail market. There are purchases I would generally classify as 'boring basics': those purchases that are more of a necessity to everyday life – offered cheaply, quickly and easily by the supermarket giants and through the likes of Amazon. Then there are purchases I would call 'interesting additions': offered by those who deliver excellent service, quality and experience. Examples of retailers in this group include successes such as Apple Stores, John Lewis, Hotel Chocolat, Lush and The Bread Shop. These are all very different stories, but all about higher-end positioning fulfilling the wants, not the day-to-day needs, of their customer. To add further value these retailers also deliver exceptional service, a great retail experience and ensure that their customers are always delighted when shopping with them. Shopping with retailers who offer the 'interesting additions' is not a chore in the same way that it is to go to the supermarket and buy the 'boring basics'.

If you want to be an interesting addition and not a boring basic then you'll need to remain focused on a high-end service positioning, however big your business becomes.

Before we wrap up on Step 2, positioning, I've got one more example to share; I mentioned it earlier. This example proves how positioning can make an ordinary product, tea and cake, worth an incredible price.

Afternoon tea at Fortnum and Mason

If you have ever had the pleasure of taking afternoon tea at Fortnum and Mason, or indeed any of London's leading hotels, you know you will pay *a lot*. You expect it, and yet you don't mind at all – this is all about the experience, and what a luxury it is! How do they manage to charge such a premium *and* be fully booked week in, week out? The answer is found when you look at my mantra about service delivery and managing customer expectations:

> When your brand makes promises, implied or explicit, these set expectations with your customer. If you fail to deliver on those promises you will fail to deliver the expected customer experience.

Fortnum and Mason consistently deliver the expected customer experience, time and time again. Their positioning makes all the promises that mean tea, sandwiches, cakes and biscuits command a price which is in the region of 400 per cent more than you might pay in a more modest cafe!

Let's explore the elements of their positioning to see how:

- **Product**: from the finest teas to the most exquisite, handmade, freshly prepared sandwiches, cakes and biscuits, *all* products are produced from the very best possible ingredients and any special dietary requirement you can think of is catered for without question.

- **Price**: 400 per cent more than a reasonable cafe; comparable to/a little cheaper than the most prestigious London hotels, eg The Ritz.

- **Presentation**: Stunning! Every single detail you might think of has been considered, from the silverware to the staff uniforms, from the interior decor to the live pianist playing delicate background music. It's like something from a bygone era.

- **Service**: Everything you would have come to expect; again every detail has been considered. Nothing is too much trouble, the staff appear just as you need them or blend into the background when you don't.

It's all very congruent; the arrows are all completely aligned. That's how you can justify an incredible price for what is otherwise an ordinary product. That's positioning.

Summing up

Congratulations, you have completed Step 2 of the 10 steps to retail success. In this chapter we have covered positioning in detail, considering the four elements: product, price, presentation and service.

By working through this step, by considering *your* business positioning compared to your competition, you may well have been able to note down some areas for improvement. Make sure you add these to your action plan.

We worked through the way that positioning can be used to attract more of the right kind of customer and to avoid you falling into the trap of trying to be all things to all people. We also looked in more detail at another trap many smaller businesses fall into; underpricing and over-serving. I've explained why that can't be profitable, or congruent to your positioning, and how you'll be far better off if you **don't compete on price, you compete on service!** Hopefully you'll be mindful of that.

This chapter also introduced a very important theme – the relationship between positioning and customer experience. Although I'm at risk of repeating myself I'll say it one more time:

> **When your brand makes promises, implied or explicit, these set expectations with your customer. If you fail to deliver on those promises you will fail to deliver the expected customer experience.**

So, you have a goal, a mission and are very clearly positioned. Generally speaking we know your positioning will be attractive to your more ideal customers, and not so attractive to others. Now, as we move forward into Step 3 we need to look at *who* that *ideal* customer is, in a great deal more detail.

Step Three
Ideal customer

Introduction

Welcome to Step 3. In this step we're going to work on defining exactly who your ideal customer is. This step builds on what we covered in Step 1, when your mission statement generically stipulated your ideal customer group. Then in Step 2 we discussed how to best position your business for success; obviously when positioning your business you'll have had an ideal customer group in mind. Now at this stage we're going to really drill down into the detail and help you to define your ideal customer *as an individual*. The ultimate aim at the end of Step 3 is to **know your ideal customer so well that they'll be as familiar to you as an old friend.**

It can often be counter-intuitive for a business owner, keen to increase their customer base, to actively plan to rule out certain customer groups. In this chapter we'll work through some of the challenges I often hear when asking businesses to be more specific about their ideal customer, and I'll share some examples and stories with you as to why this element is so key to the whole process.

Knowing and identifying with an ideal customer is one of the fundamental building blocks of the 10 steps to retail success. As we move forward into Steps 4, 5, 6 and 7 we'll regularly refer back to your ideal customer.

So, let's get started!

Your imaginary friend

Although we now have a relatively clear idea about who the customer is from the work on the mission statement and the positioning, this is not enough. From those two pieces of the puzzle you'd still not be able to recognize your ideal customer the moment they walked through the door.

I want you to get to a level of understanding about your ideal customer that makes you so familiar with them that you can describe them in as much detail as you could describe a good friend. When I speak at events I often tell the audience that they need to know their ideal customer as if they were an imaginary friend. Admittedly I get some funny looks; but as we work through this concept and begin to really describe your ideal customer you'll see how knowing them in the greatest of detail is key – and of course **your ideal customer IS your business's best friend: they spend the most, most often, and they tell everyone they know about you.** We all need friends like that in our businesses!

It can be a bit of a leap of faith. Whenever I've asked a room full of retailers, who all want *more* customers, to focus on just one, it doesn't always go down too well at first. However, by talking through some of the examples I'll share with you here they usually do come around to my way of thinking. As we go through this chapter, and work through the steps beyond, you'll realize why defining your customer in as much detail as possible will really help you. Only when you are targeting a very specific customer can you have absolute confidence that you're presenting the right products to them, at the right price, and marketing to them in the right language.

Before we dive into the detail, I do understand that for some businesses there will need to be more than one ideal customer. Depending on the breadth of the offering – the ranges available – a retailer *can* have more than one ideal customer. If that sounds like it might be applicable to you then you need to have a good justification for why you do need to have more than one ideal customer. It's hard enough to consistently deliver on your promises to one customer group; by adding more you're increasing your chances of getting it wrong, you're adding complexity to your business. Don't forget that for each ideal customer your business targets you have to be able to consistently present them with the right products, at the right price, and market to each of them in the right language. If you're not absolutely certain that this level of complexity is critical to your business success then I'd suggest that you avoid it! If you think this might apply to you I suggest you step back, really think about it, and ask yourself if you need to have that complexity. Could you simplify things? Are you making work for yourself by having more than one ideal customer to focus on? You might realize when you think long and hard about it that all you are actually doing is 'keeping your options open'. That won't help us, because as we move on we need to have been specific.

I raise this point as for so many smaller retailers this concept is so counter-intuitive that at the beginning they do try to hold on to more than one ideal customer. When looked at in closer detail most smaller retailers have a very clear ideal customer; they don't need to define multiple customers. However, I will share a couple of examples of where more than one ideal customer can be defined, in detail, and for a justifiable reason.

Being U

One of my clients, Being U, has developed a range of lingerie uniquely for 'women of colour' to provide skin tonal garments for black and Asian women. This was a sector that was previously under-served. Sadia and

Sam, the founding directors, planned to offer their product ranges both for wholesale into other retailers and for direct retail through their e-commerce and other channels. Being U have developed three distinct ranges, and as Sadia and Sam are both highly experienced marketing professionals, they defined their ideal customer not only as an imaginary friend but actually by attributing each of the three ranges to three people they knew well:

1 Teen range – for young women of colour, their mother is making the final purchasing decision, spending what they believe to be a fair price to purchase high-quality underwear for their young lady daughter. The mother is keen to ensure their young woman has a good posture, so a great fit is essential. She will choose a garment that is suitably discreet under school clothing. This is the equivalent purchase for a developing young woman to Clark's shoes for the feet!

- Sadia's own teen daughter was the inspiration for this range, and Sadia is essentially the customer (the one parting with the cash). She knows how important it is for a teenager to feel both comfortable and 'appropriate' in their lingerie choices so this range was developed entirely around a very clearly defined end user (her daughter) and purchasing decision maker (herself).

2 Core range – practical lingerie for a busy professional woman who wants natural, nude skin tones in comfortable, wearable, discreet lingerie, with an excellent fit.

- Sam became the example of the ideal customer for this range – favouring practicality and usability over flamboyance and extravagance. Practical, efficient and sensible Sam epitomized who this range was for.

3 High end – luxurious, delicate and beautiful lingerie, still tonal to the skin, simply stunning designs, and a treat to wear.

- Sadia epitomized the high-end customer; even when presented with fabrics she was naturally drawn to the most expensive! She is a lady who would choose to have a small selection of exquisite items rather than a wide choice of more ordinary garments. She works hard and saves money expressly to afford her the luxuries in life.

Being U were very lucky to be *so* close to their three target customers; however, with the two ladies' marketing expertise they would surely have either created their imaginary customer in such detail as to feel that they knew them, or identified a friend, relative or past work colleague who was the embodiment of who they were developing their products for.

I am sure you can see how, as a result of such a strong visualization of who they were developing product for, they were able to be very clear about designs, pricing, marketing and customer engagement. Essentially this customer definition primes the next four steps in the 10-step process.

My second example is based on a cafe/hospitality retail business. It's actually a 'made-up' example, but it is based on a hybrid of two businesses that do exist. I've just elaborated in order to really make the point. Maybe one day I'll start up this hybrid business myself; I can see it being a lot of fun and also very profitable!

Clare's Cafe

There was a cafe that needed to increase profitability by earning more revenue during classically quieter times. They were well set up for daytime drinks and snacks, but in the mornings and evenings they had very little business and were therefore closed for more hours than they were open. They recognized that if they could open longer hours, trade more effectively and make their premises earn more, they would be more profitable.

They observed the people passing by throughout the day and noticed that the passing customer changed significantly. So, rather than focusing on just one customer type, with one offering (as they had before) they decided to change their menus and even their 'ambiance' over the course of the day in order to extend their appeal to three different ideal customers, and of course to extend their revenue opportunities.

Obviously, as experienced cafe owners they were mindful that the key to profitable hospitality retailing was being able to serve more customers for more hours of the day. In fact, that's key to all retailing but in a hospitality environment the needs and wants of the customer do change significantly through breakfast, lunch and into dinner, and, depending on the offer presented, the type of customer does of course vary too.

So, looking at these three ideal customers in more detail:

The morning customer – Mr grab-'n'-go!

The morning customer was a 'grab-'n'-go' professional. You could easily define them if you sat and watched for 20 minutes or so – all dressed similarly, you can guess they work as lawyers, accountants, architects. This customer group all purchased a takeaway coffee with either a muffin, pastry or toasted sandwich. Grab-'n'-go. The majority of the higher spenders were men, there were women customers, but almost none of this group chose anything other than a beverage. Health-conscious, 'low-carb', professional women who like to keep an eye on their figure *do not* eat muffins, pastries or sandwiches!

This morning customer could be defined as an imaginary friend. What follows is just a made-up profile. The idea is that it will make you feel as if you really do know this customer:

> Michael is 42, a married architect who works and lives in a small city just outside London. Michael and his family moved away from the stresses of city life so that he would have a shorter commute, freeing up more of his time to spend with his kids who are five, three, and seven months. He drives his BMW estate into the city centre every morning, parks in the long-stay car park, and on his walk to work through the high street he likes to pick up his favourite cappuccino and Danish.

Can you see how you can begin to really 'know' Michael? Try and complete his profile; think of answers to these sorts of question: What is his house like? What does he do for relaxation? Where does he take his holidays? What does his wife do now? What did she do before they had kids?

It's actually about creating a stereotype that as the business owner you can really 'understand'. Once you've defined this customer you are well on your way to knowing absolutely how to service their needs and wants!

The daytime customer – Ms Yummy Mummy!

After the commuters have all got to work the high street is quiet. The shops are opening up and there are a few shop workers who stop off on the way to pick up a coffee – not many, though. This 'lull' between the commuters and the next segment enables the cafe owner to do a quick, effective and temporary transformation.

Suddenly, just after the school run is over, the cafe has become a haven for mums and childcare professionals. Now the hectic commuters have disappeared the high street takes on a more relaxed pace and ambiance; so, to fit in with the customer who is now passing by, the cafe owner changes the offers boards, the food on display, the music and quickly installs a 'kids' corner' by adding a few bean bags, a toy box and a rack of books. Suddenly what was a hustle-bustle, suited and booted, fast-food outlet is now a child-friendly cafe where people linger for hours, spending a considerable amount of money on coffee, hot chocolate and cookies. These are all low-food-cost, easy-to-serve, and therefore higher-margin items.

You can define the target customer, can't you? Have a try – I'll get you started:

> Sally is on maternity leave with her third child. She also has one child in full-time education and a toddler. Sally likes to meet her friends a couple of times a week to get a bit of adult conversation. As a break from routine she likes to get out of the house, but needed a place to go where she can relax in the knowledge that the kids are safe and can play without upsetting anyone else. In the cafe Sally can relax (and spend), knowing that she is welcome. Sally spends a great deal of money here, and so do her friends; she is a profitable, loyal, regular customer.

Have a go at writing a full profile about Sally – her age, likes and dislikes, professional/educational background, home life, what car she drives. Have some fun with this – trying to define an ideal customer for a business that is not your own will get you thinking about this in more detail so you can apply the same logic to *your* business by the end of this chapter!

Ok, back to my cafe.

The evening customer – chilling after work

By 5 pm all the 'yummy mummies' have gone home – they needed to either pick up older kids from school or get back for bath time. So now our cafe is transformed once again into a relaxed wine bar offering tapas but no main meals. With a mixture of comfortable seating and shabby-chic wooden tables and stools, funky music and a good selection of wines, beers and bottled ciders, this is the home for all young professionals after work. Drinks are high margin and very easy to serve; tapas can be prepared in advance in quieter periods during the day so as to be quick and easy to deliver to tables for snacking customers.

I'll not define the customer for this phase of opening – you should have got the picture by now. If you want to have a bit more practice at this then have a go and see what you come up with.

This canny cafe/bar owner has really understood the dynamic of the local community. Realizing that three very different ideal customers, with very different needs and wants, can be catered for by making minor changes to the offer and ambiance during the day has maximized revenue. There are lots of Michaels, lots of Sallys, lots of young professionals and importantly lots of their friends living in this area... the model is a great way to make more profit from the fixed overhead of the single cafe premises.

In my first example, Being U, the business owner was fortunate enough to be able to base their ideal customer on people they actually knew – in the second example I was making it up based on two cafes I know – one that does the morning and daytime bit really well, the other who does daytime to evening – either one of these two real-life businesses could take the third step and add on a breakfast or evening offering if they felt it was appropriate.

The key to defining an ideal customer is that it doesn't have to be some-one you know. You can make up an 'identikit customer', picking out attributes you believe are ideal from a variety of customers you already know, or you can create a whole new persona. If you can, as the ladies of Being U did, actually identify with an individual you know personally, it is considerably easier to ask yourself questions in your day-to-day business such as 'but would [customer name] be drawn to this... window display, promotion, item, marketing flyer', etc.

But I want more customers!

Earlier I mentioned that it is very important to be absolutely specific about defining an ideal customer. I mentioned how this seems a bit alarming to some business owners. When I give talks on the topic this part always causes consternation. People in the audience say things like: 'But I want to have more customers than that. I don't only want one type of customer. I want more!'

I have realized that to begin with, business owners do find this extremely counter-intuitive and really rather scary. I can see they are not buying into the idea. Even when I illustrate how they can have two or three ideal customers, like Being U or my cafe example, and how this can be based on the different 'offerings' of their business, I can still see a room full of sceptical faces, so, what I would usually answer is:

> When you are talking to one person, uniquely, about your business, about how it provides for their needs and wants, in a tone of voice so familiar to them, you will not only be talking to that one person but you'll in fact be influencing all the people *who are quite a lot like* that one person.

Of course what I mean by this is that while we are all unique we belong to a peer group who share a great deal of commonality with us. The messaging you put out will feel more personal, more 'as if it was written for me' to the reader if you write it with an individual in mind and not as if you were just broadcasting to anyone passing who might take a moment to listen. We all like to be treated as individuals, to be listened to, and to be engaged. Being talked at is far less engaging and typically turns people off.

Bear this in mind. If you write your marketing materials as a direct message to that one very familiar person, your ideal customer, then the style of writing will be more personal, more familiar and more meaningful. In this way you are more likely to capture the attention of more people, which is rather ironic! Let me illustrate this with an example:

Attracting Sue

You want to attract 'Sue'. She is 46, married with two children and lives in a five-bedroom detached house just outside London. She works part-time, but used to work in a highly paid, full-time position. When the kids are at school she is working and in her leisure time she goes to the gym or out to dinner parties with friends that she's met through the school. Her husband continues to work full-time in London.

If you want to attract 'Sue', and if you do a good job, you'll discover there are actually a lot of Sues! In addition you will also attract 'wannabe Sues' (young women aspiring to her lifestyle); 'has-been Sues' (older women who used to have her lifestyle and still enjoy many of the same things); and then all the friends and family of the numerous Sues, wannabe Sues and has-been Sues as they recommend your business.

And all you started with was Sue.

I hope that gives you a bit of confidence to trust me on this one and to start to really think about your ideal customer as a specific individual.

I can't define only one customer type – it will cripple my business!

The other challenge people throw at me about this topic is: 'But I've got several different types of customer. I can't define only one!'

My answer to this in the first place would be to **analyse your types of customer and understand which are the most profitable, loyal and most similar to the one you expected to attract when you wrote your mission and positioning**; continue to focus on that one initial type.

For the businesses who are a bit more 'evolved' in their thinking, or who have very clear offerings that support maybe two or three different, specific, unique customer groups (like Being U or the cafe example) then obviously having two or three defined customers is fine. *But not more* – because then you fall into the trap of *not* being sufficiently defined. Before you know it you'll have defined 20 ideal customers! Linked to what I mentioned at the outset, about being able to consistently deliver for your customer, there is no way that a small business can successfully deliver 20 customer propositions, 20 product ranges, 20 promotional strategies, etc. In fact there is no way that a big business could, either, and nor would they even try, so be realistic and be honest with yourself. Stick to the core customer and stay focused.

Example – focusing on the one ideal customer

I was invited to provide advice to business owners through 'surgery sessions' at an event in London in 2011. One of the people who came to see me was the owner of a family-friendly cafe on the outskirts of Bristol. He said that he had a problem with two very different customer groups. It so happened that one group deterred the other from coming to the cafe, especially in the mornings. He didn't know what to do. He really wanted to please all his customers – he had a great service ethic. With a bit of digging, I found out that his early-morning clientele were labourers. He served a huge breakfast for just £5 and they loved it. Just after 9 am the after-school-run mums turned up. Like in my earlier made-up example, he explained that these were a high-spending group who wanted easy-to-serve lattes and muffins. The business owner had already worked out that he needs these customers: they are profitable, loyal regulars. Unfortunately they felt threatened by the loud labourers and started going elsewhere. He was torn. He was falling victim to 'doing what he'd always done'. He didn't think he should change his offering and disappoint one of his customer groups, yet it was his offering that was the root cause of his troubles, the reason he was disappointing his best customers!

There was a solution.

The first thing to recognize was that he'd already identified that the most profitable segment were the mums. They were ordering high-margin, simple-to-prepare items. He was losing these customers due to the fact they felt uneasy around his second customer group. He'd also recognized the labourers were low profit – they always bought his big breakfast, which was relatively low margin at £5 and involved a lot of preparation and service.

To be honest he knew that the answer to his problems was to deter the labourers – but it felt wrong to him to actively 'put off' customers. Still, if he didn't do something he'd lose his higher-spending, higher-margin, daytime trade so he needed to bite the bullet.

Given that the labourers were attracted by the very good value for money presented to them by his big breakfast he needed to take action to reduce the value of the breakfast. He could serve the same meal for a higher price, or he could prepare a breakfast for the same price that was less substantial, and thus less attractive to that customer segment. It didn't matter which, the outcome would be that over time he would see a reduction in the number of non-ideal customers and that would be offset by an increase in the ideal customers.

It's a tough thing for a business owner to actively repel customers. It takes a great deal of courage and belief in your product and in your positioning to focus on your ideal customer. *But* if you were to analyse your business performance and identified similar issues to those faced by the cafe owner you would need to take similar actions too.

The key benefit from knowing your ideal customer is being able to understand that it is not always just about volume. In fact, the saying 'less is more' does apply. **Fewer, high-profitability, loyal customers equal less cost, less work, and more money in your pocket.** Surely that's an outcome worth aiming for?

Defining *your* ideal customer

I couldn't let you get to the end of this chapter without putting you on the spot. If you are starting up you are in an ideal place to define your customer, in detail – use the examples above and try it out. In the coming chapters you'll see the ideal customer being referenced when it comes to your product strategy, pricing and promotions, channels and location, engagement approach – having a clearly defined ideal customer is fundamental to your business.

If you are already trading you can approach this in two ways:

1 With a blank sheet of paper – define the ideal customer without any reference to your existing customer, then make the comparison.

2 By observing your existing customer base – seeing which are 'best fit' for what you envisaged when you started out in the business when you wrote your mission or developed your positioning.

The outcome of this will be unique to you. The actions you take could make a big difference *but* before you make any actions I'd recommend we work through Steps 4 to 10. If there is a mismatch between your actual customer and your ideal then over the coming chapters you'll learn some strategies to address that. The example above, the value proposition of the big breakfast, uses price-elasticity thinking. Price elasticity is covered in Step 5. So be patient, hold that thought, and as we work through the rest of the steps make sure you make some notes as to how what we work through can be leveraged to enable you to implement changes that will increase your ideal customer numbers, and reduce those who are less well suited to your offer.

Summing up

In this step I've shared with you how important it is, as a business owner, to be absolutely precise about who your ideal customer is so that you can literally empathise with them as you go about your day-to-day job of making decisions that impact them. Your ideal customer is who you are buying product for, who you are selling product to, and why you are in business – you can't afford to be vague about this!

It's not about being restrictive – it's about being specific. You'll soon realize that there are a lot of people just like your ideal customer. If you serve them well they will bring along all their friends – who will have very similar needs, wants, likes and dislikes to your ideal customer.

You also have to consider those who aspire to be your ideal customer – the wannabes! They will want to buy from you, and while they may be less frequent customers initially they might become more like your ideal customer in future and they will already be loyal to you.

Like all of us, your ideal customer ages – remember this – if they loved your offering (or would have loved your offering had you been about when it was most relevant to them) then chances are you will still be able to fulfil some of their needs and wants. I call this group the 'has beens' – I don't mean it in a derogatory way, it's a fact; once upon a time they were your ideal customer, now they have aged. While a trendy fashion boutique aimed at 20-somethings may not be appropriate for a professional in her 40s it may still stock a few items she would like – if she 'has been' a loyal and satisfied customer in her youth she may pop back and buy accessories, or something for a party... don't think this group don't apply to you – they do!

By analysing your ideal customer you will discover that by *not* being all things to all people you become a very important part of *some* people's shopping experience. Think about your own shopping experiences – with smaller or larger retailers – is there a shop where you just know you'll find exactly what you are looking for? Did there use to be a shop like that but you just 'outgrew' it?

If you can really ensure you know your ideal customer so well that you almost know what they want before they know it themselves then you are in the perfect position to secure their custom, their loyalty, their advocacy. These are all aspects that we will cover in Step 7 when we look at customer engagement.

As I said, this step will be referenced in the next four. Please make sure you have done a bit of thinking about your ideal customer before we move on. Now, if you are ready to move on, let's dig into how you develop your product strategy and how to plan your range.

Step Four
Range planning

Introduction

From the mission we've already determined the product offer, at least generically. In the positioning, we've talked about the product in terms of pricing and its attributes, but still not in detail. Now we know the customer as if they were an imaginary friend so we can buy product for them. Congratulations, we're ready for the next step.

In this chapter we're going to work to produce a range plan. To do this we're going to use the understanding we have of our customer, and either past trading information (for established businesses) or projections and forecasts (for new businesses). To get to a range plan we're going to make some strategic decisions about the range direction. We'll consider the importance of 'width vs depth' (where width is the term used to describe a great deal of choice across different categories and depth is the term used to describe a great deal of choice within a category). In the end we'll output a plan that is actionable in your specific retail space, relevant for your customer *and* which will deliver your financial business goals.

How? Well we'll look at some far more practical constraints – size of your store, category sales mix/forecasts – this is where the 'opinions' that we have formed in early chapters meet with the facts, figures, data and analytics. We'll also have a look at some of the common mistakes that smaller retailers make when it comes to selecting the products for their range and how these can be addressed.

In this chapter I will introduce some of the definitions of key 'numbers' you'll need to be keeping track of in your business – numbers that are likely to first be calculated on your range plan. These will come up again so it's important to be aware of them from this stage.

We'll wrap up Step 4 with an exercise in how to create a range plan for your retail business – something you'll probably find you can't live without once you've created it!

So, I hope you're all fired up – let's look at the first consideration in planning the range.

Who are you buying for and what do they want?

In the previous chapter I briefly used an example about a customer called Sue. To recap:

> She is 46, married with two children and lives in a five-bed detached house just outside London. She works part-time, but used to work in a highly paid, full-time position. When the kids are at school she is working and in her leisure time she goes to the gym or out to dinner parties with friends that she's met through the school. Her husband continues to work full-time in London.

Sue will be the ideal customer in this example. Now that we know that Sue is the ideal customer we need to identify products to sell that Sue will want to buy – and knowing Sue so well we've really got some clear boundaries.

Imagine you are out at a trade show and looking at items. If you knew you were selecting a range for Sue you would be able to quickly rule in the products that you believe she will most want to buy from you. You can put yourself in her shoes; consider what Sue would favour in terms of style, function, occasion, price point, choice. You might also think about who else she buys for. Depending on what your retail offering is it may be relevant to include some items that Sue might purchase on impulse – items that she would pick up as gifts for her children, friends, family, etc.

So, let's work the example of our customer through
Let's assume that today Sue would like to buy shoes – and since Sarah Decent runs a shoe shop, let's imagine that Sue is going to Modish. Sue is a good customer for Modish – very close to ideal – so this example should be quite realistic!

Sue is keen to buy shoes that are good value for money and comfortable. It is important that her footwear is suitable for her busy lifestyle *but* she's a stylish lady, she won't choose comfort entirely over style and nor does she want to make a fashion faux pas. She's buying something she can wear both for work and at home; she mainly likes to wear trouser suits and jeans – so in her mind's eye she is thinking she'll probably make a beeline for the ankle boots. That's her perfect solution for her autumn/winter requirements and a versatile option for both work and home.

Now, let's look at the retailer side. If Sarah wanted to buy a range of shoes for Modish, and if Sue was the ideal customer that she had in mind, what would she go for? In the past, without following a clear product strategy and not using a range plan, she might have selected too many options that fulfilled the same basic customer need and not have budget or space in the shop to allow her to offer a wider selection. For instance, she might have bought into a large range of court shoes, leaving little space for ankle boots. Thus, when Sue comes in to buy ankle boots, the choice is too limited. She doesn't feel the shop's range is sufficiently broad, there is too little on offer to get her attention, thus she continues to shop around. She walks out empty-handed – that's a lost sale. The fact is, Sue had come into the shop to buy ankle boots – that was what she felt she most needed. When she discovered that the range, the choice presented to her, wasn't broad enough, she's walked away with nothing. If the range had been sufficiently wide, with more choice, more to browse, more products likely to be 'just what she was after' she might have bought a pair of boots (or two) as well as something else that just happened to catch her eye. If that had happened she'd have left the store feeling that she had had a very successful shopping experience, no time was wasted, she'd got what she wanted (and more), and was happy. When customers like Sue have good shopping experiences they come back. In Sue's case time is precious; she has a very busy life – a retailer who makes it easy for her to find what she wants will quickly make her a loyal customer.

So Sue became a loyal customer because the right range was an important part of the customer experience. In Step 7, customer engagement, I'll explain in more detail how the right range contributes to the attraction, conversion and retention of customers... as it did with Sue.

Back to Modish; Sarah has implemented a range-planning process for Modish and as a result she has a well-defined, relevant product offer. Sales are up, stock obsolescence is down, and her customers keep coming back. She has told me that she uses the range plan religiously when going to the trade shows to ensure she's got a framework to work within when building a range for the forthcoming seasons.

Sarah's range framework, from which she builds her range plan, is based on some of the facts that she knows about her business constraints. She knows that she has a finite number of products that she can fit into her retail space; she understands the categories of product that her ideal customer will expect to see; and she understands the sales mix in each of these categories and so she can allocate the right balance of space and number of products to each category. We'll explore *how* she knows all this in the next section.

From all of this insight Sarah knows that she should ideally have say 10 choices of ankle boot on offer for her ideal customer. (I'm using example numbers here, not her actual data.) She knows which colours, styles and shapes she needs to choose in order to ensure that those 10 items do make a customer feel that there is a credible choice on offer. What would the outcome be with Sue? Well, when Sue comes into the shop there should always be at least two or three out of the 10 options presented that she would like to try on – she feels she's been presented with a great choice, she might remark that she is 'spoilt for choice'. She feels happy, the experience is exciting – and a relief too because she won't have to waste her precious time shopping around. Modish make shopping fun and fulfilling, not a chore – and Sue is very grateful for that – she'll certainly be recommending them to her friends! From the range presented she can make a shortlist of her favourites and try them on. Really, at this point a sale is only dependent on availability of the chosen item in the right size. If Sue can justify the expense she'll probably buy a couple of items – thinking that if she can't choose between them, she'll just have to have both, it'll save her time in the long run! She won't be walking away empty-handed because there was a relevant, appropriate and credible offer presented. Well done, Sarah, a triumph for Modish and Sue is a happy, loyal customer.

Range construction

You probably noticed in the example above I rather glibly gave a long list of details that Sarah would know about her range that led her to know she should have a choice of 10 ankle boots on offer.

In this section I'm going to explain how she knows. Taking each statement individually I'll explain how you too can build your ideal range framework. This is the starting point – and I use the terms range framework and range architecture interchangeably. This is what you can take out with you on your buying trips and visits to trade shows. You would populate the framework with the products that you have in mind for the range to ultimately create your new range plan for the forthcoming season, just as Sarah now does.

1 How many products can you present in your store?

This requires you to take a good look at your store – you need to make a realistic assessment of how many unique products (known as SKUs – stock-keeping units) you can merchandise in your store.

If you are a clothing or footwear retailer you'll work at option level – essentially this is style–colour level – as in how many unique garment options your customer would choose from. Your SKU-level detail would be style–colour–size. While you do have to plan your stock, and record your sales, at the SKU level of detail you don't have to merchandise every single piece of stock on the shop floor. So you work at the level at which the customer notices the product, the option level – eg red wrap dress, blue wrap dress – two options (style–colour variants) of the style wrap dress. The SKU would be red wrap dress, size 14.

When you've assessed what we can call your SKU count (clothing/footwear retailers read 'option count') you have an overall maximum range size for your physical space.

It's critical that you know this because this is how many items you'll be aiming to include on your completed range plan. Too many and you'll struggle to get them all on the shop floor – ending up with a cluttered space or, worse, items not on display (and they can't sell from the stock room). Too few and you'll unnecessarily restrict the choice you are presenting to the customer, and you may lose customers because you're not presenting either sufficient width or depth in your range; you will not look sufficiently authoritative in the categories you are presenting.

You can of course extend the range you offer should you have a strong e-commerce presence – and we'll cover that in more detail in Step 6 – channel and location. For now, let's assume your primary sales channel to be your store; hence you need to build the ideal range for that store space.

Now you have a reasonably accurate SKU/option count determined you can move on to the next question.

2 What categories does your ideal customer expect to see?

Think about what you've claimed in your mission statement and your positioning. Think about what kind of offer your ideal customer would expect you to present to them. Now you can begin to list the categories they would expect you to offer. Here's an example: If your mission is to offer an 'authoritative range of home decoration items' and your positioning is to offer 'luxury home decoration' then it naturally would suggest an ideal customer who has a high level of disposable income, who cares about her home (and yes, it ought to be a female) and who probably is an 'empty nester' (anyone with kids will know you don't buy luxury home decoration items when you've got a toddler on the loose).

The choice of the major categories that could be offered is entirely up to you, the retailer. These are just a logical way of grouping items. Ideally you would use categories that align to your customer's decision tree; that is, the process they go through to decide what product they eventually want to purchase. Using the customer's decision tree is useful when it comes to visual merchandising, because you can merchandise a product category together, making a logical display of 'solutions' to 'consumer needs'.

An example of categories and subcategories belonging to the category for the home decoration example could be:

- wall-mounted items – mirrors, picture frames, wall art, shelving;
- soft furnishings – cushion covers, curtains, rugs, throws, bedding, table coverings;
- ornamental – vases, free-standing pieces (interior and exterior), candle holders.

The crux is that you are making logical groupings of products based on the similarities they have in function/end use or purpose – in a similar way that a customer might shop.

Consider this scenario. A consumer is thinking the wall in their hallway looks a little bare. They pop into their local independent interiors shop for some inspiration – at this point they're looking for product that could be used to make the wall look more appealing but they have no fixed ideas about what that might be.

On arrival in the store they see the 'wall items' presented together in an engaging display – these items could all add interest to that bare wall and include a variety of mirrors, wall art and picture frames. Immediately adjacent are wall shelves – interesting, but in this case the consumer rules them out – the hall would feel too narrow with anything that dominant. The customer continues to browse the products that are most appropriate to their needs and ends up selecting a mirror.

Sometimes the consumer decision is quite generic. There are times when the decision process is more specific – beginning at the subcategory level. For example, if you receive flowers and don't have a vase to put them in then the next time you're at the shops you'll specifically be looking to buy a vase!

Whether the customer's mission is generic or specific, by now you should have clearly thought out the 'groupings' of products you'll sell, and also those you would not sell. Now you can apply some science to this step, which has been more about having a good understanding of your customer, your market and their expectations, than it is about the figures! Fear not, the next step is all about the figures.

What is your forecast sales mix by category?

You've got your product groupings – categories and subcategories. Now you need to use some insights to apply a forecast sales mix. The insights can be based on analysis of your past sales, a view from information provided by suppliers, knowledge you've gleaned from speaking to customers, from attending tradeshows, or from specific research. However you get to the insight it is important to ensure that the sales mix by category (the share of total sales that each category will take) is realistic. Don't fall into the trap of basing your estimates on history alone either – you need to be mindful of the future shifts in consumer demand and trends to ensure you increase your presence in categories that are growing and reduce it in categories that are in decline.

Once you are happy that you've got a sales mix by category that is logical, based on knowledge, experience and insights, *and* relevant for the future, then you have all the initial information you need to develop your range construction.

So, therefore, what is your range construction?

At this point it's really just about applying some 'fair share' logic. Let's walk that through:

- You know what you expect each category to deliver in terms of contribution to sales – so you know the mix.
  - You ideally should allocate your space based on a similar fair share; better still if you can allocate space based on margin share – if you can; do so.
- From this you know that a category delivering 25% of sales (or indeed 25% of margin) will be allocated 25% of merchandisable space.
- You also know the maximum number of items (options or SKUs) that you can merchandise in your store over all.
- Thus, by taking that same fair-share thinking and applying it to your overall item count you now also know the maximum number of items you should be planning for per category – it will be 25% of the total.

Simple, really! This gives you the framework for the range – estimated sales (and margin) per category, space allocation and target item count. It's somewhat simplified *but* it's a framework and that's all you need to begin to develop your range plan.

Before we move on to that, I wanted to share some of the common mistakes smaller retailers can fall foul of.

Common mistakes

Most of the smaller retailers I speak to who struggle to achieve their top-line forecasts don't have that framework, the range architecture, that we have just worked through. Without this as a control tool they have nothing to guide them (other than gut feel and past experience) when selecting products. They fall into the trap of buying on a whim – whatever catches their eye; or buying a repeat of something that has done well before. This can cause problems. So, ahead of creating your range plan the table that follows identifies some of these common mistakes, the impact these can have on a retail business, and how you can avoid them.

TABLE 4.1   Common mistakes in selecting a range, the potential impact on your business, and how to avoid making these mistakes in future

The mistake	The impact	How to avoid
The retailer buys what *they* like, without a customer in mind.	You'll only appeal to customers who are just like you! If that's a good-sized market then you're lucky, but you won't be necessarily meeting your goal, mission or positioning *or* fulfilling the needs and wants of your 'Imaginary friend' if you've not bought for your customer. Moreover, if you don't buy for the ideal customer and end up not selling the product you've purchased then you'll have all your cash tied up in stock that's not selling – a sure-fire way to get into very bad financial shape very quickly.	Use Steps 1 to 3 to ensure you have a thorough view of the customer. Then complete Step 4 to build a range architecture template. Use that to give you something to refer back to at trade shows/buying events and to avoid being drawn in by products that *you* like but which don't have a place in your ideal range construction.

TABLE 4.1 *continued*

The mistake	The impact	How to avoid
The retailer buys product at a price that doesn't allow sufficient mark-up. (Thus, should they need to clear the stock by having a sale or promotion, they end up losing money.)	Mainly financial – not dire, but could have been managed differently. You'll likely break even on the overall product purchase as sales at full price will offset the cost of clearance, but it's unnecessary to give up margin this way.	The calculations and explanations of terminology in the latter part of this chapter should help you better understand the point at which you would 'walk away' from a product. You need to be certain that you can retail for the RRP and that the buying price gives you sufficient margin. You can always look for better products to invest in. **Remember, the products on your range are investments** – you've got a maximum number of products that you can physically fit into your retail space, not to mention a finite amount of cash that you can afford to tie up in stock. **Each product (investment) needs to really 'earn its keep' and provide you with a sensible return**. A product can provide a return on investment either directly – by bringing in great margin, selling in good volume; or indirectly – by being an enticement into the store and thus a contributor to a larger overall spend by your customer. In Step 8, on sourcing and supply chain, we will take a look at some options that may be available to you when it comes to supplier negotiations, when trying to increase your margins to ensure you have enough 'room' to allow for discounting should you need to clear residual stock of an item at the end of season.

TABLE 4.1 *continued*

The mistake	The impact	How to avoid
The retailer buys quantities that are too great or too little. Thus they sell out of some lines and are left with residual stock to clear of others.	If you've under-bought you'll have lost sales and potentially frustrated customers who really liked the item but were unable to get it before you sold out. If you've over-bought then you'll be left with residual stock that you'll need to either carry forward onto the next season's range plan (thus removing the chance of bringing in new lines at possibly better margin) or you'll have to reduce it to clear if it doesn't 'fit' with the next season's range – thus delivering a lower than ideal margin unnecessarily.	There are several strategies to avoid this issue – many of which we'll explore in more detail in Step 8 on sourcing and supply chain. The key to this is, however, to have a very realistic planned rate of sale in mind for the products when you buy into them – and you should plan to sell out at the point in time when stock of new items arrive. I can guarantee you'll get it wrong; a forecast is always wrong! The more accurate you are the less risk there is in terms of lost sales or overstocks. When we come to Step 8 bear in mind we'll also look at the opportunities to negotiate purchasing arrangements with suppliers that enable you to be more responsive to consumer demand. This section will touch on a range of buying terms that you might be able to negotiate with your suppliers that really do help to de-risk your stock-buying process. These include ordering smaller, more regular replenishment quantities on sale-or-return agreements. If this is an area where you need a bit of extra help make sure you spend a good deal of time and focus on Step 8!

TABLE 4.1   *continued*

The mistake	The impact	How to avoid
The product range doesn't give you a price ladder to climb up. All your products are of an equal value, not presenting a choice from 'good–better–best'. There is no opportunity to 'upsell' a customer by taking them from a solution that meets their needs to a solution that is more desirable and retailed at a higher price.	If you've got a range of choices but with no apparent price difference the customer may find it difficult to differentiate between items, become confused, and buy nothing! You also reduce your opportunity to increase your average transaction value by taking your customers up the price ladder – which is explained in much more detail in the next chapter; Step 5, pricing and promotions.	If you want to have an authoritative range for your ideal customer, particularly if your strategy is to present depth (lots of similar items, a specialist retailer) as opposed to width (lots of different items, a variety retailer) then you do need to show you've catered for their needs and wants. You need choices for when they're feeling like splashing out, *and* for when they're feeling a bit strapped for cash – it's important to recognize that even your ideal customers will sometimes prefer to spend less on an item and at other times will feel at ease paying more. To really engage the customer you need to ensure that the range is built not only with the pure product architecture in mind (the construct of categories, numbers of options/SKUs, etc) but also with the appropriate price architecture in mind – aligned to your positioning. If pricing is an area where you struggle then make sure you dedicate some time to the next step as well!

So, now we're clear on how to create a range framework and how to avoid common mistakes, it's time to have a go at it.

Creating your range plan

When you think about it, a range plan is actually an incredibly simple tool, but incredibly effective. At the end of this exercise you'll not only have the beginnings of your own range plan, including a better understanding of all the terminology, but you'll also be in a much more confident position when it comes to trade show season!

Terminology

Let's first take a look at terminology. There are certain words, especially around the figures, that I will refer to with regard to the range plan. This terminology is commonly used and you will hear it from your suppliers. In my experience many of the retailers I speak to are not that clear about what it all means. Some are confused about the 'deal' a supplier is offering as supplier A may express their deals as 'enabling the retailer to mark up by X times' whereas supplier B might say 'meaning a margin opportunity of Y per cent', but not be clear as to what version of margin they mean. The trick is to have a simple calculation tool to hand, I would suggest an Excel spreadsheet is as good as anything else, that enables you to work out what these statements mean to you in cash terms. The explanations below should help you to do that.

Simple terminology explained:

- **Retail sales:** This is the amount of cash you've taken, net of returns, but inclusive of VAT.
  - This is a useful metric – if you measure your retail sales daily, and also record the total number of transactions, you can work out your ATV (average transaction value). Sales and ATV are good measures to use to set targets for your staff. It will encourage them to deliver the best possible total customer experience – from making sure stock is on display and correctly priced, to offering good advice about items if required. Only by working as a team and delivering great customer service will they increase sales. Setting targets with the team, and incentivizing them to deliver those targets as a team, will encourage them to work together to deliver the best experience for your customer. Knowing that sales are net of returns will discourage them from the 'hard sell'; because if a customer feels they actually didn't really want something that they were 'sold' they'll simply bring it back.

- **Net sales:** This is the retail sales value as explained minus VAT (where VAT is payable on the item in the first instance – one to watch if you sell certain items with zero VAT such as children's clothing or reduced-rate VAT items such as mobility aids – check the details with HMRC in the UK).

  - **Net sales** are expressed minus VAT as obviously the VAT is cash you owe to HMRC on your next VAT return due date and is not cash that belongs to your business.

- **Cost of sales/product cost:** This is the total cost of the goods, minus VAT, that were sold to achieve the retail sales value. Ideally the cost price you use for this calculation is the 'landed' cost – meaning the cost of goods including delivery to your location. If the cost price that you buy products from suppliers at does not include delivery then you need to apportion the delivery charges across all the products on the delivery to give you a more accurate cost price per item. Obviously you can't receive the goods without incurring a delivery charge, thus it is a direct cost of sale.

  - **Note:** Cost of sale is expressed *net* of VAT payable on your purchases as at your next VAT return date you will either receive a rebate or make a payment based on the difference between VAT owed to HMRC (from retail sales) and VAT due back to you (from purchases).

- **Cash margin:** This is the difference between the net sales value and the cost of sales value. This cash essentially is the true income to the retail business from which all fixed and variable operating costs need to be paid for before you can calculate your profits. Cash margin = net sales – cost of sales. There are two ways in which the cash margin can be expressed as a percentage margin – and it is critical you know which you are dealing with.

  - **percent margin GMROI:** Gross margin return on investment. This is the cash margin expressed as a percentage return on the original investment in the stock. I find this formula useful: percent margin GMROI = (net sales – cost of sales)/cost of sales.

  - **percent margin of sales:** Gross margin achieved on sales. This is the cash margin expressed as a percentage of the net sales. Essentially it states how much, as a percentage, of the net sales value is the margin income for the business. I find this formula useful: percent margin of sales = (net sales – cost of sales)/net sales.

This is confusing; so to put this in numerical terms to make it absolutely clear:

1 Net sales = £100
2 Cost of sales = £50

Therefore:

3 Gross margin = £50

4 GMROI margin = 100% because on an investment in stock of £50 the margin return is £50.

5 Margin of sales = 50% because on a sale value of £100 the margin return is £50.

I hope that makes it clearer – I found it confusing when I first came across these two measures, and as people just say 'margin' it can be hard to know which version they mean. Suppliers will do this, so ask them to clarify what exactly they mean.

- **Mark-up:** This is another area where many retailers I speak to are confused. Mark-up is also expressed by some suppliers as 'coefficient of retail' – regardless of the way in which it is expressed, essentially this is the multiplication factor that could be considered a reasonable 'rule of thumb' to apply to the landed cost price of a product (the price of the product delivered to you) to determine the ideal retail price. Sometimes this is expressed inclusive of VAT, sometimes not – watch out for that!

Mark-up example: If you are at a trade show you need a calculator on hand. Here is a scenario to work through:

- A supplier quotes you £10 ex VAT landed cost for an item.
- This item is subject to VAT at retail.
- Your target ex VAT mark-up is 2.

So, on your calculator you are tapping in:

- £10 × 2 (that gives your ex VAT retail price, equal to the landed cost × mark-up).
- Next, depending on the VAT rate, let's assume 20% for simplicity of the numbers, you multiply by 1.2 (to allow for the uplift of the retail price due to VAT at 20% in this example).
- The resulting target retail price is £24 including VAT.
  With a starting cost of £10 sometimes this can be expressed as a mark-up of 2.4. That's because the mark-up is being expressed at the full retail price including VAT. At other times it is expressed as a mark-up of 2, because that's the net (ex VAT) retail price. I think this inconsistency in the way mark-up can be expressed is the main reason why people get confused. Make sure you know which version you're working with.
  Back to the trade show, the next consideration is to decide if this £10 item can be retailed through your shop for the target of £24. If not then you'd have to make a judgement call – is this product so

critical to your range that if you didn't have it you'd lose customers? Can you find a suitable alternative that will achieve your target mark-up? Of course, you don't have to retail it for just the £24 either; this is only your target retail price. You can choose to retail the product at £29 or £35 if the market will tolerate that price. If you can increase your target mark-up then you've bought well. As long as you have confidence that the product is suitable for your positioning and for your ideal customer then you are well within your rights to charge as much as you see fit for an item; it'll compensate for the items that you don't make target on.

That's the key terminology that you need for your range plan explained, and some of the outline calculations. We'll use this in the actual example we'll create, but before we move on to that I'd like to make a quick point about VAT. If you aren't already registered, or if you are a start-up, you should speak to HMRC or your accountant about when you should register for VAT. In my experience you should register asap as you can claim back all the VAT on purchases and costs in your set-up stages. Beyond that there are two VAT schemes – the regular one (you pay VAT on sales and you recover VAT paid on purchases) or the flat-rate scheme. Bear in mind HMRC can change the schemes offered at any time. You may find that you are better off on one scheme or the other. You can investigate what works best for you with a couple of simple scenarios; whichever you choose you are entitled to change your scheme if your business dynamics change and it makes sense for you to do so.

Your range plan: what it looks like

A range plan can include as many columns as you feel are relevant to the analysis of the plan – so if fabric is relevant to your customers' choice, and ideally if you have past data that shows the sales mix between fabrics, then including that as an attribute on the range plan is a great way to make sure that when subtotalled by that attribute, the mix is in line with your expectations.

You need to ensure you have a row on the plan per SKU/option.

On the next page is a simplified example of a range plan for the category 'ankle boots'. It's not based on any real figures; it's just an example.

If you want to download a more complete range plan template in Excel, populated with all the formulae and some example figures, you can visit **www.retailchampion.co.uk/resources** – it's called 'template range plan'. I mentioned the resources area in the Introduction. Access to the resources area is usually exclusively offered to my clients, but I've decided to open it up to all those who read this book. The first time you visit the resources page you will need to complete the form on the right, including the access code from the front of this book, to request your log-in PIN. As soon as you are issued with your PIN you will gain the same level of access as any of my

TABLE 4.2 Example range plan template

Category	Sub-category	Colour	Finish	Attribute	Landed cost (ex VAT)	RRP (inc VAT)	Net margin	GMROI	Mark-up inclusive VAT	Average week rate of sale
Ankle Boot	Flat	Black	Leather	Zip side	£30	£69	£27.50	92%	2.3	2
Ankle Boot	Flat	Black	Suede	Stretch	£36	£79	£29.83	83%	2.2	2
Ankle Boot	Flat	Brown	Leather	Zip side	£29	£69	£28.50	98%	2.4	1
Ankle Boot	Flat	Red	Leather	Zip side	£32	£69	£25.50	80%	2.2	0.5
Ankle Boot	Heel	TBC	Leather	Stretch	£32	£75	£30.50	95%	2.3	2
Ankle Boot	Heel	TBC	Suede	Zip side	£34	£79	£31.83	94%	2.3	1
Ankle Boot	Heel	TBC	Leather	Laced	£33	£85	£37.83	115%	2.6	2
Ankle Boot	Heel	TBC	Suede	Embellished	£37	£89	£37.08	100%	2.4	0.5

clients, free of charge. With this you will be able to download a variety of tools, templates and calculators that are mentioned throughout this book.

The range plan will eventually include every single option/SKU that you plan to have available on the range presented to a customer who walks into your store. In a 'live example' you may not have fully populated all of the information. This is a document that evolves from a simple outline structure when you are planning a future season through to a plan you can literally place your initial order quantities from.

In the example on page 66, I've assumed that we knew the items in the 'flat' subcategory but in the 'heel' subcategory we were making estimates – thus we're targeting an RRP, based on an appropriate price point and price ladder. Then we're planning a landed cost based on that RRP and the target margin. This means that in a negotiation with a supplier you're able to refer to the range plan, consider your target retail prices (drawn from your price architecture, which comes up in the next chapter), and say 'Ideally I don't want to pay more than £X for that item – is there anything you can do for me?' You never know, there could be manoeuvre in the product cost price; for example if you placed enough orders to achieve a certain volume threshold with the supplier you might get the price you wanted.

Also in the example above there is a low rate of sale on the red, flat ankle boot – which also delivers lowest net cash margin – nonetheless, if red was predicted to be the 'in colour' in the current season it is a necessary addition to the range. Your range could look incomplete or 'not current' without it. The benefit of a range plan is that when faced with decisions such as 'Should I stock the red boot?' you have the prior expectation that it will deliver a lower margin and rate of sale, so as a result you can be conservative about the order quantity that you place to avoid getting caught out with excessive residual stock.

Worth noting is that the retail price for the flat, suede boot is £10 higher than the other leather options – again, the suede boot is an example of a price ladder – where a customer might trade up to a more 'luxury' fabric for a higher price. Perhaps the next 'rung on the ladder' is a knee-high boot, or a heeled boot – price ladder is something we'll cover in the next chapter in a lot more detail.

Anyway, I'm sure with the example on page 66 you can easily see how by playing with the formula and numbers you can develop the outline range structure into a comprehensive buying plan.

Let's look at what else you might do with this tool.

What to do with your new range plan

I've mentioned trade shows a great deal – I guess it won't come as much of a surprise to you to know that the best use of your range plan is to ensure what you select at the trade shows delivers your business goals and isn't just a collection of stuff *you* like!

As you can imagine, with so many great new products all under one roof, the trade shows are designed to inspire you – but don't be seduced into buying more than you need – you can't stock everything! You should use your range architecture to help you to decide which products you want to consider including in your range (pending supplier negations – Step 8) to make sure you have what your customers want, what will realistically fit in your store *and* that will deliver on your financial targets.

As you walk the floor of the trade show ask yourself: 'Do these new products match with my ideal customer's expectations?' and 'What purpose would this product serve on my range?'

Somewhat rhetorical perhaps; you'll intuitively know the answer *if* you've done the preparation work and created an outline range structure as a minimum. That range architecture will form the basis for the final range plan, and having used the insights from Steps 1, 2 and 3 to ensure that the product is in line with your goal, mission, positioning and customer expectations you're bound to be onto a winner!

Next, you have to remember that you have a finite amount of space and ensure you stick closely to your total option/SKU count. If the new items within a category would be ideal for your offer, but there is not sufficient space to effectively merchandise them, you need to make some choices and either de-list a less ideal product from that category, or 'steal' options/SKU count from another category to make way for the new item.

If you are already trading through stock from a previous season, or have some residual stock to clear for this season, you may need to include these items as 'carry over' on your range plan. This suggestion would not apply to very specific seasonal products, eg Christmas decorations. While this approach takes SKU count away from your new range it does avoid the cost of discontinuation. If, however, you are sitting on a pile of stock from this season, not appropriate for carry forward, that won't sell through before the end of season, you can really only do one of two things:

1 discount it to clear; or

2 put it into storage and bring it back out for the same season next year.

You need to decide which is more prudent financially and in terms of the offer for the customer – if they recognize you're selling the exact same Christmas stock this year as you were last year then they'll not be too impressed; although they might never notice if the stock is mixed in with enough new items!

You need to consider the financial implications too – clearance will reduce your margins but will put cash flow tied up in old merchandise back into the business, meaning you can re-buy with that cash. Hopefully when you re-buy you'll choose items that will sell through and deliver you better margin next time around. Storing stock will cost you more money *and* keep the cash flow tied up, but if that means you can sell the stock next year at full price, and generate sufficient margin to justify the decision, then it's a good alternative. Finally, the range plan works in tandem with your price architecture – you'll have to consider how the products you select fit into your price positioning and how they work together as a price ladder – all of this will be explored in more detail in the next chapter, Step 5, pricing and promotions.

Overall range planning touches on the retail disciplines of buying, merchandising, pricing, space planning and stock planning. What you present on your shelves, and how you present it, are the outward representation of what your retail business stands for in the eyes of the consumer. Essentially the range is three out of four elements of your positioning – the product, the price and, depending on how you come to merchandise it in store, the presentation too. You need to consider the role each product plays on your range, the impact of adding new products and de-listing others, and the reasons why you are making changes to your range. If you use range planning effectively then you'll arrive at the best decision both for your business and, most importantly, for your ideal customer.

Range planning: robust and repeatable?

In the last section of this chapter I want to just have a quick sanity check at this point, before moving on. The reason I've written this book, the reason you're reading it (I hope!) is that I wanted to share some insights into my 10 steps to retail success process that enables retailers to develop robust and repeatable processes (and systems) in order to become scalable, saleable businesses.

Sound familiar?

Great – but look at the above so far... very useful I am sure you'd agree. Likely to make your business more profitable? Certainly. However, at no point, yet, have we added how you can make range planning a robust and repeatable process.

The key to this will come from some level of systemization. So far, we've assumed you can access data and information about your current business performance but we've not considered how easily, or indeed how accurate it is, let alone how long it takes.

Once you've established a process to set your product strategy, to analyse your past range performance, and to develop your range plan for future seasons, you need to consider how to make that faster, more efficient and, most importantly, how you could delegate that task to a buyer. One day, as your business grows, you'll need to pass this process on to someone you employ specifically to develop product strategy, range plans and to manage the flow of merchandise into your business. Thinking ahead, how could that be made easier?

You need to free up your time to create a platform for growth; you don't need to be the bottleneck to the process. To do so you will need to consider investing in systems (if you don't already have something in place that can be 'tweaked'). Ideally you need an EPOS (electronic point of sale – which is a great deal more than just a till system) to keep track of sales. EPOS will additionally enable you to manage stock and to report on a wide range of facts about your business. At the touch of a button an EPOS will provide you with reports on daily sales, number of transactions, average transaction value, what items are often purchased in the same transaction... in fact, if the raw data exist you can develop a suite of reports that allow you and your staff to really understand your business performance at a glance.

Most modern EPOS systems will also integrate with most e-commerce platforms; so if you run an online shop this allows you to have just one master system where you set up all your products and prices – a further time saving.

Finally, a good EPOS will also provide you with the majority of reports you need for financial accounting, management accounts and, critically, the data on which future demand forecasts can be based.

So, if you don't have EPOS and you're serious about making your business a success, I'd urge you to look into it – there are so many options available – do your research, think about your requirements, talk to other retailers. In Step 10, back office, we'll cover IT requirements in more detail, including some advice about selecting appropriate, 'future-proofed' business systems.

When you do have EPOS, all of the analysis I've described above – to determine the ideal space allocation per category based on sales (or, better still, margin) mix; to determine the average rates of sale per week for an item... and more... are all very easily created as reports from your data – so quite literally your customer will be telling you their needs and wants, based on what they've purchased before. All you have to do is apply some insight to the forward planning of your business – meaning the analysis and decision making can be done relatively quickly and with confidence that all of the decisions being made are based on facts and not assumptions or guesswork.

Clearly, the first time you undertake the process it will be less accurate, but if you consider that your journey will be one of continuous improvement you'll find that the second and third times you go through a process you'll do it better. Over time you'll become more accurate and more efficient. By adding appropriate automation and systemization into your business you can free up your time to focus on building your retail empire – based on the strong foundations of robust and repeatable processes and systems.

Summing up

Congratulations – you've completed Step 4, range planning. This step is really at the heart of retailing – after all, it's all about the product! Step 4 is central to the 10 steps to retail success process, translating all of your thinking about goal, mission, positioning and ideal customer into an actual, executable range plan. This range plan details at option/SKU level how your choices of product will match back to your higher-level forecasts and projections… but how? A quick recap.

Well, we've walked through the thought process behind the outline of the categories you plan to sell and how your sales forecast should be 'shared' out between the categories based on the mix you are planning for each of the categories to achieve.

We've also considered, based on the physical constraint of your store size, how many 'choices' (options/SKUs) overall you can realistically and effectively merchandise – meaning that when customers browse they can actually see the whole range.

From those two estimates we've been able to determine not only a sales mix per category but also an item count per category. This is the basis for your range architecture and provides you with a very clear set of boundaries when visiting trade shows or going on buying trips so that you can avoid many of the common mistakes.

I've highlighted the important role that Steps 5 (pricing and promotions), 6 (channel and location) and 8 (supply chain) will play in terms of influence to the range plan, and in the avoidance of many of the common mistakes. Range planning is an iterative process, eg learnings from Step 8 (Supply chain) may mean that you make updates to your range plan – and this is quite normal. The plan is there to help guide and steer you prior to making final commitments.

Then it was over to you – to actually think about creating your range plan – the template supplied should have got you started. In my experience not one of the retailers I've worked for ever had an identical format to their range plan, so it's up to you to evolve it into a planning tool that supports your business needs and your decision making.

Finally we looked at how, as a pivotal step in your 10 steps to retail success, range planning needs to be fed with dependable, accurate information for it to really work – and thus touched on how by leveraging EPOS you can access more accurate insights about your business performance to enable you and your team to take quality decisions, ensuring you've got the right indicators about past performance to repeat success and to eliminate issues in the future.

So, the next overlay to your range plan is your price architecture, and that comes from your pricing and promotional plan. The target retail price for items will enable you to begin to review margin per item, rates of sale, return on space and ultimately to make decisions about products not only on gut feel but also on facts that mean you will know that you will make some money – which is probably one of the fundamental reasons why you are in business in the first place! Let's get started then; Step 5 is pricing and promotions.

Step Five
Pricing and promotions

Introduction

We've touched on pricing in the positioning step so we know roughly where we are positioned on price relative to the competitive set. We also know our ideal customer and thus their spending power. We understand what the ideal customer would perceive to be 'value for money'. In the last chapter we have worked on developing a range plan; so we have a view of the products we plan to offer, what they cost, and the margin/mark-up we're aiming to achieve.

So, really, shouldn't pricing be just based on that? Isn't it just about applying the mark-up to the cost price of the product and presenting the items to the customer?

Unfortunately it isn't quite that simple. You could do it that way, but that's not going to underpin *successful* retailing!

In this step we're going to work through how pricing and promotions tie back to your positioning – and how, if you get your pricing and promotions wrong, you could be sending out confusing messages.

Next we'll look at three powerful concepts when it comes to pricing:

1 price elasticity;
2 price ladder;
3 assortment elasticity.

And we'll consider how these influence your price architecture.

Finally we'll look at different promotional mechanics, why to run promotions, and how to create a promotional calendar.

At the end of this chapter you should:

- understand the relationship between the customer, the product and the price points;

- be able to get started with your own price architecture and apply that to your range plan, developing it from an outline plan to a much more detailed tool;

- be clear as to what the right promotional mechanics are for your positioning and customer, and be able to create your own promotional calendar.

So, let's get started with Step 5 of the 10 steps to retail success process.

Impact of price and promotions on positioning

You'll have considered price as part of the step on positioning. When it comes to actually setting price points you need to make sure that you stay in line with the positioning you've developed, otherwise you'll confuse customers. Remember that if you present an upmarket, glossy brand, and offer a fantastic product and service, you *must* have a higher price point in order to cover the costs of the other three areas. Don't forget the very clever strapline used by Stella Artois, 'Reassuringly expensive': this is so true. People assume if something seems too good to be true then it probably is. When your pricing seems too low for what you offer you will end up making your customer suspicious, potentially putting them off buying from you. I am sure you've also heard the statement: 'It's too cheap – something must be wrong.' It is. Your positioning arrows aren't aligned.

Reflect on Step 3 – think about your ideal customer – you want to attract the right kind of customer, one who matches your positioning. Price is of course one of the most telling statements about 'where you are' in the context of the market.

To stay true to your positioning you need to be clear about your price strategy, how you will handle discounts and clearance, and how you will undertake promotions.

One of my clients had a product that was very much a higher-end offering. On her website she was presenting her end-of-line items with 'big red sale' styling. The presentation looked cheap – incongruent with otherwise opulent and luxurious branding. The price was heavily discounted, making the full-price items look decidedly expensive.

Since pricing is an element of positioning it is fundamental to the impression you give. You can still offer 'good–better–best', where these represent choices of increasingly good quality within the range. Don't forget, your ideal customer's perception of acceptable pricing for a product that meets the 'good, better and best' logic will be very different if you have arrows down vs arrows up in your positioning.

Carry this through with promotions. If you have arrows down then you can easily carry off clearance discounts and the 'big red sale' image. If your arrows are all up, as was the case of my client who had used 'big red sale' discounting for her end-of-line products, it simply doesn't work.

Promotions for 'arrows-up' brands need to be more creative – still offering good value and an incentive for the customer to purchase, but remaining congruent with the arrows-up positioning.

Some of the ideas I discussed with my client included:

- Don't slash prices – give customers voucher codes to be redeemed on specific (clearance) items – the customer feels that it is a little more exclusive.

- Package up bundle deals on lines you want to sell through – offer a collection of products typically purchased together for a special price that represents a desirable discount.

- Offer link-save or multi-buy deals on lines you want to sell through to reduce the unit price to the consumer; stimulating demand, but without the appearance of item discounting.

- Make specific products 'featured', eg product of the month. By highlighting an item in-store or on the front page of your website you may never need to change the price and yet you'll still enjoy uplifted sales!

- Set up an eBay shop or Amazon marketplace, possibly under a different brand name. Make that your clearance channel, and sell only end-of-line and clearance items through this channel. You can then specifically position this channel as your clearance outlet and not negatively impact the primary brand positioning.

So long as you are clear on your price positioning from the outset you'll be able to have far greater confidence in your pricing strategy and approach to promotions. That strategy will prime the next step of the process – determining your price architecture.

Price architecture

Price architecture is similar to your range framework, in that it is a structure that you use to define your pricing. It has some influence over the final products selected for the range as it will be necessary to consider those in the context of your intended price architecture – these two steps, 4 and 5, are very much interrelated and iterative – so when you come to work through them in practice you'll probably find yourself bouncing between your range architecture and price architecture. The result will be a complete range plan that meets your business goals.

Your price architecture should include three ingredients:

1 price elasticity;

2 price ladder;

3 assortment elasticity.

We'll work through each of these to explain what role each aspect might play in your retail business.

Price elasticity

You are probably familiar with the term – it's a standard term from economics. It's about the relationship between the price of a product and the number of customers willing to purchase it.

Price elasticity is the factor that explains the relationship between the price of an item and the impact that has on demand. In layman's terms, more often than not, this means that the higher the price the lower the volume.

Fuel (petrol/diesel), for example, is highly inelastic. Almost regardless of the price per litre, consumption remains very consistent. That's because there is a high dependency on fuel for transport. Conversely, a product with a very elastic price might be a piece of jewellery. As the price point increases you will see a proportionate reduction in the volume of sales.

Price elasticity is used by luxury brands that set 'prestige pricing' for an item, thus making it exclusive because the majority of consumers can't afford it. At the other end of the spectrum supermarkets are driving high-volume sales by keeping the prices as low as possible.

In the context of your retail business price elasticity is one way in which you can influence the amount of volume you sell of an item. I'm sure you'll be well aware that volume increases when the price decreases – but do you know by how much? By analysing and recording the amount of discount offered and the associated uplift in demand you can use this insight when you need to clear product at the end of season. Let me explain.

Assume that you've got six weeks to go before your new products arrive. At that point you'll want to merchandise your new range in your store. An item on the current range isn't selling as well as expected – in fact at the current rate of sale you've got 10 weeks' worth of stock to sell through. That means residual stock of the item will be hanging about four weeks into the launch of the new range. It will be taking up space where you'd be better off merchandising a new item, and the rate of sale may slow down even further when new products are available. What do you do? You could discount – but by how much? Twenty per cent? Thirty per cent? Fifty or seventy per cent? How far do you cut the price in order to stimulate the demand and achieve sell-through in six weeks? Not sooner, or you'll have a gap on the shelves; not longer, or you'll have overlapping merchandise.

Well, clearly you have to have some insight from past discounting activity to provide you with this information – and that's why price elasticity can be important to you in your business. If you knew that a 30 per cent discount on that type of item would be sufficient to accelerate the rate of sale then you can get away with that discount and not have to go as far as 50 per cent – which would both give up margin unnecessarily and potentially achieve the sell-through too quickly, meaning a gap on the shop floor.

Another way that you can use price elasticity logic to your advantage is if you are in short supply of a desirable item (assuming that item cannot be purchased from elsewhere). If you increase the price by 10 per cent you can reduce the demand. You won't sell through as quickly *and* you can increase your profitability as well.

Price ladder

A price ladder is literally the stepping-up of price points within a selection of products that ultimately fulfil the same 'purpose' for the consumer. On the price ladder each item represents a slightly better value proposition (better features, better quality, etc). Most retailers offer some kind of price ladder. Retailers who understand their positioning should have prices that offer their target customers choice within their budget for products that meet their shopping mission. A price ladder can also be described as presenting choices from 'good' (meets consumer requirements), 'better' (is an enhancement, something extra) and 'best' (is top end). With good–better–best the value-adding attributes of each item become more compelling as the price increases, thus you take your ideal customer up the rungs of the price ladder.

Think about this with regard to Tesco own-brand food, for example – you have Tesco Value (good enough for their customer), Tesco standard product (better than value) and Tesco Finest (best they offer). However, the overall positioning for Tesco would mean that the customer attracted to Finest would still be unlikely to do their weekly shop at Waitrose; or, to put it another way, a loyal Waitrose customer is unlikely to consider Tesco Finest 'best' compared to their expectations. In the context of Tesco's pricing the Finest range represents a luxury item to their customer base. To the loyal Waitrose customer it might appear average. So, you can see how this 'good–better–best' price ladder still has to meet the expectations for *your* ideal customer as defined by your positioning.

The reason a price ladder works so well is that your customer thinks that the entry price point item, the 'good' item, is OK – they'd have been happy with that. When they see the 'better' item and think 'Ooh – that's worth an extra £X' they have started climbing the ladder. If you then show them the 'best' item they'll be delighted – and certainly keen to climb to the next 'rung'.

Of course, it doesn't continue indefinitely. What typically happens is that the customer aspires to a rung where the price point is simply too high; they don't feel that it is 'justifiable' for their budget. At this point they will usually drop back to the rung of the ladder they can afford, or which they perceive to best meet their value expectations for the item.

Here are a couple more examples where price ladder is used very effectively:

Example 1: Car industry

The car industry uses price laddering extensively and effectively. There is a basic model at the entry point, and then different models of the same type, built on the same chassis, at each stage up the ladder. Of course, with each step up the ladder you get more 'bells and whistles' included, and once you've decided you can't live without rain-sensitive wipers there is no dropping back to a more basic model! The customer, who might have got everything they *really* needed in the basic model, can swiftly find themselves actually wanting to spend considerably more because of all these additional features.

Consumer behaviour is typically to start at the bottom of the ladder; then they talk themselves up to the rung where they are actually uncomfortable with the price; so they then take just one step back.

Example 2: IKEA

In IKEA the way that their products are merchandised on the shop floor is carefully planned; and it is based on the price ladder. Think about a fixture as innocuous as 'tableware'. Basic white plates are merchandised at the first part of the fixture that you arrive at. As the customer walks along the shelf, usually from left to right, they are introduced to products that have an increasingly good quality or finish; and of course the associated higher price. IKEA are actually turning their price ladder into a method of visual merchandising. At each step along the fixture you see a product just ahead of you, in your direction of travel, that represents a slightly more desirable option, at a slightly higher price.

How to implement an effective price ladder

If you want to implement a price ladder in your retail business there are a few key things to consider:

- The price range (minimum to maximum) that your ideal customer would be willing to pay for this kind of item.
- Setting the prices so the steps between price points (the rungs of the ladder) are fairly equally spaced – and then trying to ensure all the items in your price ladder are delivering a consistent per cent margin of sales, or an increasing per cent margin of sales as the retail price increases.
- Merchandising the products within the price ladder so that the entry price point item is placed at the part of the fixture that the customer

would naturally arrive at first. This will depend on the customer flow through your store. Immediately adjacent to the entry price point item you should merchandise the item that represents the next rung of the ladder, and so on.

- Make sure the product packaging and/or POS (point of sale/in-store signage) clearly explains the additional value-adding attributes to the customer if this is not abundantly clear. A price ladder is far more effective if the consumer moves up the price points based on their own judgement of the product value. Well-utilized point-of-sale materials replace a salesperson in the process and ensure that the customer feels they've arrived at the up-sold decision with no active selling from a third party.

To find out if a price ladder could work for your business you need to try it out – only through trials will you really be able to understand how well your customer will respond to your price ladder. In the most part a good price ladder, clearly presented, well merchandised with effective use of point-of-sale materials, *will* enable customers to up-sell themselves with no intervention from sales staff – what retailer could ask for more?

One more point, touched on above: the price ladder is most effective when your percentage margin of sales on all of the products in a range of 'comparables' is pretty much the same; or greater the higher up the ladder you go. The reason for this is that the cash margin you realize on an 'up-sell' (up the ladder) increases proportionally to the increased retail price. If that's not the case, then assortment elasticity might be your answer.

Assortment elasticity

First of all, for the avoidance of doubt, 'assortment' means the items from a range that are visually presented for sale to a customer in your store or online. If you have more than one store, or a store and e-commerce, you don't have to have exactly the same products presented to the customer. Big retailers buy a whole range of products and then plan which assortment (selection from the whole range) will be presented in which of their stores. Smaller stores get a reduced assortment; larger stores get a wider assortment. In your business, assortment and range may in fact be one and the same; but this doesn't have to be the case. In fact, in the next step, Channel and location, we will talk about different products selling in different channels – and hence I wanted to introduce the term assortment in order that we can refer to your range as the entire selection of products that you buy and the assortment as the selection of products that you present to the customer through a channel or outlet.

So, now you know the difference between range and assortment, we can look at what assortment elasticity is.

As we discussed earlier, price elasticity is relevant to the single item; but price elasticity can also have an influence across an entire assortment.

Therefore I use the term assortment elasticity essentially to describe the way that the price points within an assortment of similar items influence the behaviours of consumers.

If the assortment includes three or four items that could satisfy the consumer's needs, and likely as not includes a price ladder, you'd be forgiven for thinking you'd done as much as possible to optimize the opportunity to sell. Almost, but not quite! Assortment elasticity is all about changing the 'distance between the rungs' on the ladder; about varying the incremental price from item to item to influence a consumer to buy the item that gives *you* maximum margin.

Admittedly it takes a bit of thinking through – the first time I came across this concept I had to sit and work it through in my mind. To bring this to life I'll illustrate this concept with a cheese grater! This is a real example from a major retailer.

Assortment elasticity example
In a supermarket non-food section there was a choice of four cheese graters priced 99p, £1.79, £2.49 and £2.99 – basic, good, better, best. This was a proposition that offered a good choice and something for the wide range of customers they served.

Unit sales of all four items were about the same and per cent margin of sales on all items was also about the same. The category team were tasked with increasing the cash margin contribution for this range.

There are really only two ways to increase cash margin return on the cheese grater assortment:

1 Price elasticity of an item – reduce price and hope that the increase in volume is sufficient to cover the cost of the reduction *and* to deliver a net increase in cash margin; or

2 Influence customers up the price ladder.

The first method was trialled. The price of the entry price model was reduced to 79p. This did increase volume, but not in the way the supermarket commercial team had hoped. Due to the now more significant jump from basic to good (£1 difference where it had been 80p before) the entry price point item started to take sales away from the next rung of the price ladder. Although when sales performance of the now 79p item was reviewed in isolation it certainly was achieving sufficient additional unit sales to pay back the lost cash margin, this was at the detriment of the £1.79 item. Commercially this was a major issue. Those additional sales, coming from the higher-priced item, were now delivering a considerably lower margin. This meant that the overall impact on cash margin delivered by the assortment was reduced. Not good, and the opposite of what the intent had been. Customers traded down because compared to the whole range of cheese graters presented the 79p item offered such good value for money they couldn't really justify the higher-priced item – it was over double the price to trade up. A major gap in the thinking in this example is that the commercial team hadn't considered that consumers don't typically 'stock up' on cheese graters – they are relatively inelastic in terms of pricing (if you need one you buy one, if you already have one the price isn't going to encourage you to buy another). The assumption that a reduced price would encourage incremental sales was an error of judgement in this case – one to consider, because when it comes to some items in *your* assortment you won't always be able to increase demand by reducing the price.

After that disastrous trial a second approach was tried. This time the decision was taken to *increase the price* of the entry model to £1.29. This might have reduced volume, and the commercial team were concerned that it was a bit of a risk. However, as established above, people only buy a cheese grater when they need one, demand is quite stable. If you've got 'cheese grater' on your shopping list and are in the supermarket you'd find out that the entry price point was £1.29. You'd not know if that was good or bad – you don't buy cheese graters very often. A cheese grater is not a KVI (known value item – items that consumers have a good idea as to what the price should be) and so there is little risk of the slightly increased price point being a barrier to sales. With this in mind the price increase was implemented.

The results of this trial were fascinating, and demonstrate the power of assortment elasticity very well. When sales of the entry price point item were analysed there was a slight reduction in the number of units sold following the price increase. The risk of a negative effect on demand due to an increase in price appeared to have been confirmed. However, as every unit was now delivering 30p more cash margin than previously, the overall cash margin was about the same as it had been before.

That wasn't the end of the insight; what was so interesting in this example was *where* the lost sales from the entry price point item had gone. When the overall performance of the assortment was reviewed there was an uplift in unit sales of the £1.79 item that was almost identical to the unit sales seemingly lost from the now £1.29 item. You see, as the gap between the rungs of the ladder was now just 50p, customers felt that it was very sensible to trade up; the price difference for the upgrade item seemed good value for money. So although on first glance this second trial appeared to have stood still on margin, while losing volume, that wasn't the case. Now, as it was more compelling to step up the ladder, consumers were trading up more readily. In fact there was a very evident cash margin benefit. Not only did the item with the increased price achieve pretty much the same cash margin as it had done before, from lower volumes, but the item above it on the ladder benefited from an increase in volume such that it also delivered more cash margin. The overall result was that the total assortment produced more cash margin from the same unit volume. Excellent. The commercial team had met their objective of making the assortment more profitable and the customer was happy as the assortment still presented a choice – basic, good, better and best *and* with the change in the size of the steps on the price ladder more customers enjoyed a better-quality product as well.

It was a smart decision on the part of the commercial team to increase the entry price point product to £1.29; but they very nearly overlooked the whole picture because they were not looking at the dynamic within the entire assortment.

This example illustrates that it is not just the price of the item but also the prices within the assortment, and the relationships between them, that can make all the difference.

So, considering these three elements – price elasticity, price ladder and assortment elasticity – you need to create a price architecture that is relevant to your positioning, your customer, your financial goals, and that works harmoniously with your range plan.

Creating your price architecture

Some retailers, such as 99p Stores, are 'single price point retailers' – they don't have to worry about price architecture. They just need to continue smart buying to ensure that they can procure a credible range for a buying price that means they can retail at 99p and still make some margin. These stores are in the minority; for most retailers it's important to consider the price architecture *before* finalizing the range plan and making your purchasing decisions.

This was touched on a little in Step 4, range planning; now we need to look at this a little more closely.

On the next page is the very simplified range plan we used in Step 4; this time I want to focus on the retail prices.

In the 'flat' subcategory there are three options all at £69 – the reason for this is that they are essentially identical, save for being different colourways. A consumer doesn't care that the retailer pays a different cost price for the different colourways; they expect to pay the same price for the same item regardless of colour.

There is also a suede item for £79.

There isn't much of a ladder here, but then this is only an example plan. Even so, a £10 increase from a £69 purchase to trade up to a product that looks/feels better isn't a big difference; the customer may choose to step up the ladder.

Next, look at the heeled products – these are TBC for colour as they are 'planned' items – and there is a distinct ladder – £75, £79, £85, £89.

Without facts – analysis and insights from past trading or trials – you'll not know what effect the price architecture has on rate of sale *but* what you can see in the heeled range is that the ladder is 'lumpy': differences are £4, £6, £4, £6. Now this might be a decision to use 'psychological price points' (it is accepted that in general a customer will feel better about £79 than £80 even though they *know* it is only £1 difference), but you might be creating a barrier for the customer to make the jump from £79 to £85. If you decided

TABLE 5.1 Example range plan from Step 4 with price ladder highlighted

Category	Sub-category	Colour	Finish	Attribute	Landed cost (ex VAT)	RRP (inc VAT)	Net margin £	GMROI %	Mark-up inclusive VAT	Average week rate of sale
Ankle Boot	Flat	Black	Leather	Zip side	£30	£69	£27.50	92%	2.3	2
Ankle Boot	Flat	Black	Suede	Stretch	£36	£79	£29.83	83%	2.2	2
Ankle Boot	Flat	Brown	Leather	Zip side	£29	£69	£28.50	98%	2.4	1
Ankle Boot	Flat	Red	Leather	Zip side	£32	£69	£25.50	80%	2.2	0.5
Ankle Boot	Heel	TBC	Leather	Stretch	£32	£75	£30.50	95%	2.3	2
Ankle Boot	Heel	TBC	Suede	Zip side	£34	£79	£31.83	94%	2.3	1
Ankle Boot	Heel	TBC	Leather	Laced	£33	£85	£37.83	115%	2.6	2
Ankle Boot	Heel	TBC	Suede	Embellished	£37	£89	£37.08	100%	2.4	0.5

to make all the 'rungs' of the ladder equal, with a £5 gap then you could analyse whether that had any effect on your demand at each 'rung of the ladder'.

The key to price architecture isn't about getting it right; it's about getting it good enough and then testing some variations to determine what impact that has on your customer. As every retailer, and indeed every retail shop (even if a second or third outlet for the same brand), has a slightly different customer then I can't give a fixed formula for your price architecture. You will need to think about the elements we've covered so far and ensure your price architecture provides a framework of information about target retail price points. When it comes to populating your range plan you can consider what RRP you need to include within any category/subcategory and, in the same way as you'd ensure you had the right mix of styles and colours, you can also ensure you have the right mix of price points.

Planning of promotions

Of course, once you've got the price architecture sorted out and everything is ticking along beautifully we have to mess it all up with promotions!

Consumers do expect retailers to have promotions – and while some mechanisms will be about giving away margin to stimulate demand there are promotions that don't erode margin and yet still satisfy the consumers' hunger for a deal.

At the beginning of this chapter I outlined some of the risks of running certain promotions, especially in the context of devaluing your brand/product offer or positioning. We'll reflect on those in a little more detail in the promotional mechanics section to follow.

Before we dive into *how* to promote we need to consider *why* promotions are important, to your business, to your customer, and what impact that has on your planning/budgeting as well.

Importance of promotions and planning for them effectively

Retailers use promotions to draw attention to their stores, to their products, to drive footfall, and to increase sales. There are planned and unplanned promotions. Planned promotions are those you include in a 'promotional calendar'. These take advantage of other seasonal activities or events. These promotions are expected; you might even buy specific merchandise for a planned promotion.

Unplanned promotions are exactly that; you won't know the details about unplanned promotions very far in advance. While you would be wise to include an allowance in your financial plans for the cost of addressing slow-selling items, you won't know what items you'll be promoting, or when you'll need to take action, until you identify something as a slow seller.

These 'unplanned promotions' are so called because they are typically tactical, happening in-season, as and when required. They are usually used to mitigate the risk of an overstock if a product isn't selling as well as anticipated. Very occasionally you might be contacted by a supplier who needs to stimulate their demand; they may offer you a deal to take stock at a reduced price specifically so you can 'promote' it – retail it at a special offer price – to help the supplier sell through. These are also unplanned promotions, but beware of these – you can find yourself getting seduced by the deal and not taking the time to think it through. When presented with this kind of 'deal' from a supplier just check:

- Have you got space in the store to merchandise the product?

- What effect will a deal like this have on other products similar to it – think assortment elasticity – will it draw demand away from other products and cause you a slower sell-through on a similar item?

- Is the product suitable for your customers and will they want it at all? Will your customers respond to the deal or will you end up stuck with the stock that your supplier couldn't sell?

If you're comfortable that your supplier's offer to run a promotion is going to benefit you then go for it – if in doubt, walk away!

Another reason why you should have promotions is that consumers expect you to, especially at certain times of year such as Christmas and summer when the traditional 'end-of-season' sale is epidemic in the high street.

No matter how hard you try you can't avoid promotions; but you can use them to your advantage.

As touched on above, it's critical to ensure you include promotional activity in your budgeting. Budgeting for promotions is not only about the product margins and discounts; it is also a key element of your marketing budget. Often promotions are less about the price cuts and discounts than they are about creating some excitement around a product/range or a sense of urgency to buy an item while it is still available.

If you allow some budget for visual merchandising, window dressing/ window posters, in-store signage and creating an in-store feature, you can draw a lot of attention, create a sense of 'newness' about the in-store display, and feature products relevant to the 'theme' of the promotion, without actually having to do much in the way of discounting.

However, consumers are smart and when the rest of the high street is offering discounts, deals and offers you will have to follow suit otherwise you'll look out of place. So, when it comes to your overall business planning and forecasting you do need to estimate that only 70 per cent of the buy quantity of each item will sell at full price, with say 20 per cent selling at a reduced price (a mix of promotions and clearance) and potentially 10 per cent not selling at all or only recovering its original cost price.

We touched on this when talking about margins and mark-ups in the previous chapter.

So, you have thought about *why* you are promoting and what impact that will have on budgets, now we'll take a closer look at *how* you can create a promotion – the promotional mechanics, including a bit more on each of the methods mentioned in the early part of this chapter.

TABLE 5.2   Some typical examples of promotional mechanics, the pros and cons of each and examples of when each is best used

Promotional mechanism	Pros	Cons	Best used
X% discount on an Item	No messing about – comes straight off the price. Linked to price elasticity – usually there is a clear uplift in sales (where pricing is elastic/product is desirable).	Direct hit on margin. Consumers might struggle to calculate the actual discount in cash terms. Not generally a good idea if you plan to go back to the full price afterwards. Messes the price ladder up for similar items and can have doubly negative effect on assortment overall, as with the cheese grater example.	When delisting a product from the range – end of season/clearance. Can be used for items that aren't in perfect condition *if* you choose to sell these (think positioning – think about alternative channels for substandard/clearance goods to separate the customer and not erode your brand positioning).

TABLE 5.2 *continued*

Promotional mechanism	Pros	Cons	Best used
X% discount off a range (for a period of time/event-based)	Similar to item % discount, only across a whole selection. If you make it a 'time-specific' offer you add a sense of urgency *and* have justification to put the prices back again afterwards. Increases sell-through – useful if a range of items is not performing as well as planned. You can optionally choose to extend the offer beyond the period if you haven't sold through, or you can simply have a 'while stocks last' approach. Impacts the entire price ladder equally when applied to a range, thus doesn't create the double-negative effect.	Can irritate customers, especially if they purchased an item before the discount event – they may complain! Direct hit on margin.	To take advantage of a calendar event that might drive footfall anyway – but *don't* promote items that will sell anyway (see example below) – promote items that otherwise might not benefit from the increased footfall and only if you need to increase sell-through.
£X off an item	Similar to % discount – simple, clearly understandable. Directly linked to price elasticity, so should increase volume sales.	Direct hit on margin. Like the % discount messes up price ladder and assortment elasticity – so watch out again for the double-negative effect. Like % discount, difficult to justify returning to full price.	When delisting a product from the range – end of season/clearance. As mentioned above, can be used to sell imperfect goods, if you are comfortable with that.

TABLE 5.2   *continued*

Promotional mechanism	Pros	Cons	Best used
Vouchers (can be any kind of promotional mechanic; the key is that it is only offered to voucher holders)	The customer feels that it is a little more exclusive – 'they have something special'. Vouchers are usually time restricted and create a sense of urgency. You can give vouchers specifically to those customers who spend most/are most loyal – so it is more targeted. Vouchers can be used to capture customer details too – if you want to boost your e-mail list or postal marketing, a voucher that can only be redeemed when a customer provides their details gives you a great resource for remarketing.	Can become viral if issued online – this could also be considered a pro, depending on what you want the outcome to be! There is a cost of production as well as the margin impact at redemption – you need to budget for this.	To tie in with calendar events and occasions, especially if you want to drive traffic to your store to encourage browsing of ranges that are 'classically' associated to an event/occasion. If you have a customer database you can also use vouchers for their birthday, wedding anniversary, child's birthday, etc – be inventive!
Bundle deals (something of lower value is included when a higher-price item is purchased at full price). This also applies to free gifts, eg buy two items from a make-up range to receive a bag and several samples free	Increases the value of a package of items by including an item free when purchased with something else while avoiding a direct price discount. Definitely one that can be done just for an event/ while stocks last – so you can easily return to 'full price' as you never were seen to offer a reduced price in the beginning.	Only really works if the included item is usually purchased with the larger item – eg buy a laptop and get a printer, scanner or digital camera free – this makes sense, but buy a laptop and get a toaster free: that's a bit more random! Only really helps tip the balance for a customer who already wanted to buy the primary product in the first place – so less of an incremental sale and more of a 'good reason to buy now/ buy here'.	A good use could be if a supplier has offered an item at a preferential price and to encourage sales of a high-margin item. Can additionally be used if you have known-value items or products that are available from other retailers – if you know other retailers are beating you on price you can offer a bundle to improve your 'value' position.

TABLE 5.2 *continued*

Promotional mechanism	Pros	Cons	Best used
Link-save (buy one item to get another half price and similar)	Similar to bundle deal, only the second items are only discounted when purchased with first. Increases basket size.	More complex to manage (unless you have a good EPOS). Gives away margin on second item only.	Similar to bundle offers.
Multi-buy (buy two and get third free; BOGOF, buy one get one free)	This is all about volume, so good for clearing stock quickly. Encourages bigger basket size.	Only works when the items are likely to be needed in quantity by the consumer – not suitable for items a consumer would only need one of. Represents quite a significant discount, so margin impact can be high.	This is all about volume – so only relevant on items that a customer would 'use up' or need many of. Can be used at any time; a good tactical promotion mechanic.
Featured product – not a discount, just a 'fanfare'	No margin is given away. Great if you want to be noticed for a particular item/brand/range.	Customers might not consider it a promotion so response rate might be low. Unsuitable if you need to clear stock.	Good if all you want to do is draw attention to an item, perhaps because it has good margins.

Promotional mechanics

There are various methods of promotion that are used in retailing. Whatever you do, make sure that the offers and deals are clear to the customer – you don't want customers complaining that they are confused by your pricing or feeling misled. Every year the media get hold of stories about retail promotions; we hear how they are so very confusing, how consumers are 'tricked' into spending more money. Whether there is any substance in these stories or not, the net effect is that the consumer is increasingly cautious and distrusting of retailers and promotions. You can't afford to alienate a customer with confusing promotional information; so take care to make sure that however you choose to implement your promotions the offer/benefit is clear to your customers.

In the table is a list of possible promotional mechanics for you to consider; it is by no means an exhaustive list, but should give you a good flavour of the options available. I've also worked through the pros and cons of each type, and when each type is best used, so that you can consider each in the context of your ideal customer and positioning.

As already touched on, if you are concerned about clearance and the impact of discounting on your customer/positioning then you can develop an alternative channel specifically for end-of-line items. We will cover this in more detail in the next step.

As the table shows, most price-based promotions can help clear excess stock, but potentially divert sales away from other items in the process. Almost all promotions do involve giving away margin. When you think about promotions for your retail business work out what is best for you. In the final section of this chapter I'll show you how to create a simple 'promotional calendar'. This is a great tool that you can use to plan the whole year. You can look at the events, occasions and seasonal influences that impact your business, and decide what promotional activity, if any, you will get involved in to benefit from those 'occasions'.

Too much promotional activity can have negative effects on your business. Before we move on to the promotional calendar I wanted to share a couple of examples from larger retailers I've worked with that demonstrate this.

Example 1: Safeway fresh poultry

A buy-one-get-one-free offer on fresh chicken. In 1997–8 I was working as a lowly supply-chain planner for Safeway supermarkets. The buyers regularly ran a buy-one-get-one-free (BOGOF) promotion on fresh chicken breasts. Of course this product can be frozen and does get consumed; thus customers were able to stock up, buying three or four weeks' worth of their usual consumption when the items were promoted. It got to the point that customers were wise to this regular promotion and almost no sales were made when the chicken breast was at 'normal' price.

By running this promotion so regularly the Safeway buyers had created a customer expectation; and the customer refused to pay full price, holding off on their purchases and waiting for another BOGOF.

That wasn't the only issue. I sat on the supply-chain side. A smooth supply-chain flow aids planning for everyone – the farms that supplied the chickens, the packaging companies that prepared the product for our shelves, the transport providers that delivered it, the warehouses that stored it. The buyers' excessive promotional activity, and the impact that had on consumer behaviour, created a 'lumpy supply chain'. This meant that when on BOGOF we'd have to ship three to four weeks' worth of 'normal' demand around the supply chain; when not on BOGOF the demand dropped so low that it was practically non-existent. Consumers didn't need any more chicken breast – they'd filled their freezers up when it was promoted; thus all that these promotions did was create waves of demand that put pressure on the whole of the supply chain.

To be honest, we'd have been better off offering a long-standing discount on the items *or* being on promotion all of the time!

The final impact was that our supply chain was flooded with associated chicken products when the breasts were on promotion – drums, thighs, wings – and as this was fresh produce there was only so much that could be sold within shelf life. So, the 'by-products' of the chicken breast promotion created a surplus of other fresh items, which then had to be frozen. As you might know, frozen meat is usually sold at a lower price than fresh; thus we also lost out on the margin on those items too!

All in all, and on reflection, the Safeway buyers had got trapped into a promotional cycle that was negative for the business. The key lesson here is to avoid setting up a promotional plan that creates a 'lumpy supply chain'.

Example 2: Thresher larger promotion
Thresher were an off-licence retail chain known for their constant promotions (three for two on any wine, ongoing) as well as famed for their e-mail vouchers that rapidly went viral (40 per cent off wine or champagne). Typically these promotions were fine as the price point for a single bottle of wine or champagne was quite a bit higher than the supermarkets anyway, and as they were local convenience retailers they didn't really need to compete on price. But they thought that they did.

In 2007 I was doing a piece of work for the new CEO, Yvonne Rankin. She'd been brought in by the new owners to help deliver a turnaround as the business was not performing well. The remit was to review the business areas of range and space planning, promotions and supply chain to see where 'quick wins' could rapidly contribute to the turnaround.

One area I was looking into was the supplier relationships and specifically how Thresher might be able to work more closely with suppliers to better understand the customer. One supplier was a *massive* organization; they owned a vast array of very well-known cider, beer and lager brands. They came in for a meeting and presented some stats about sales, price, margin, etc. They had collected the EPOS data from Thresher's 1750+ stores and analysed it in detail to support the category management team in their decision making.

When we saw the graphs there was one aspect that really stuck out – right at the point when demand was climbing to a seasonal peak (end of May bank holiday, exactly when customers were all buying lager, beer and cider for their barbeques) a price promotion had been applied to some of the most popular product lines. The sales history showed a very slight increase in sales due to the price promotion, but the margin figures showed a distinct dip.

When we remodelled the sales and margin assuming no price promotion had been applied, we did see that the demand was slightly reduced. Margin, however, was much improved. The customer was going to be buying the product anyway – it was on a seasonal climb. As a convenience off-licence there was no need to be price competitive with supermarkets – if you'd just run out of beer at your barbeque you'd not jump into the car and drive to Tesco, you'd pop down to the nearest local shop.

Working with the supplier data I was able to show Thresher how promotions of this nature were an unnecessary reaction to the supermarkets, and how by running these promotions they were simply giving away profits.

So, in summary, badly thought-out promotions usually have two negative impacts. One pulls forward demand, which would have happened anyway, both giving away margin and creating a 'lumpy' supply chain. The second, where offers are placed at peak selling periods, is tantamount to just giving away margin right at the time when you had the best opportunity to make some money.

Avoid wasting opportunities for your retail business to make margin – promote as and when necessary, and not as Safeway and Thresher did, because they thought they had to.

Creating a promotional calendar

In the last part of this chapter we're going to look at how you can create a promotional calendar to help you determine when it is best for you to run planned promotions. Unplanned promotions, by their very nature, can't appear on your calendar. However, if you notice that you need to increase sell-through on some lines then at least you can tie an unplanned promotion into the planned promotions. This will mean that the unplanned promotion benefits from the expected uplift in footfall and sales that the planned event would achieve.

The template on the next page shows a few examples of content that you could have on your promotional calendar (UK specific, based on 2012); then you need to determine if you run any kind of event, activity or promotion to coincide with the calendar entry.

On your own version of the calendar you would overlay your promotional events (and can even include simple things such as a change of window feature) to fit in with a calendar event – as per the example given.

In addition to national events, if there are local or regional occasions that would affect your business and your customer, you should include these when you build your own promotional calendar.

The above calendar is just an example; but hopefully it should give you an idea as to how to create one for your business. There is also a downloadable version of this template in the resources area, if you want a head start – **www.retailchampion.co.uk/resources**; it's called 'template marketing and promotional calendar'.

TABLE 5.3 An example promotional calendar

MONTH	Calendar events	Academic calendar	Other religious holidays	Sporting events	PROMOTIONAL ACTIVITY
January	New Year	Back to school			End-of-season sale
February	Valentine's	Half term			Valentine's window feature
March	Mother's Day				Mother's Day window feature
April	Easter	School holiday – Easter		London Marathon	Price promotion – make your money go further in school holiday theme
May	2 × bank holidays	Half term			Re-merchandise to focus on high-summer items
June	Queen's Diamond Jubilee			Wimbledon	Voucher promotion for loyal customer; celebrating the Jubilee
July					Two-month event in store, windows and range of special offers about the Olympics and end-of-season sale
August	Late summer bank holiday	School holiday – summer	Eid	London Olympics	
September		Back to school			Back-to-school window
October	Halloween	Half term	Diwali		Halloween and Bonfire Night window
November	Bonfire Night				Christmas window
December	Christmas	School holiday – Christmas	Hanukkah		Gift promotions – tactical, as required!

Summing up

That completes Step 5, pricing and promotions – and congratulations, not only have you completed Step 5, but you are also now halfway through the 10 steps to retail success!

In this chapter we have worked through how your pricing and promotional approach needs to align to your positioning to avoid confusing your customer, or attracting the wrong type of customer.

We've worked through the three concepts of

1 price elasticity;

2 price ladder;

3 assortment elasticity.

Along with some examples we have considered how these three ingredients should influence your price architecture, and how that feeds into your range plan.

Then we've looked at promotions, reviewing a number of promotional mechanics, and finally we've looked at how you can create your own promotional calendar.

In the next chapter, Step 6, we'll look at channel and location – because now you know what you're going to be selling (range plan) and what price you'll be selling it for, we need to know where you're going to be selling it from.

Step Six
Channel and location

Introduction

First of all, congratulations – you're now over halfway through the 10 steps to retail success and each step is building on those that have gone before to create a robust basis for your retail business.

In this step we'll be looking at your channel and location strategy. By channel I mean the different routes to market, the different environments and methods for reaching new customers. In modern retailing it is expected that you will offer customers access to you through multiple channels. An effective retail proposition with multiple channels is called multi-channel retailing; but there is a big difference between being a retailer with multiple channels and being a multi-channel retailer. Ahead of the discussion about what channels are relevant to your business, and why, I'll explain the thinking behind this multi-channel concept. If you can build your business from the outset to offer a truly integrated multi-channel experience to your customer you'll be future-proofed and leapfrogging some of your larger competitors!

Next we'll move on to look at what might make you consider offering multiple channels. Leveraging what we know about the customer we'll be able to make some educated predictions as to which channels will work best for you based on where and how your customers would most like to shop. I believe that **it's your responsibility as a retailer to be where your customers are,** as much as possible. I don't want you to fall into the trap of just assuming they'll come to you. We'll then discuss what ingredients you might consider including in your multi-channel retail proposition, and why – these might include:

- stores (including market stalls and concessions);
- e-commerce (including mobile and apps);
- party plans;
- consumer events (fetes and fairs, occasional markets and shows);
- catalogues: mail order/phone order;
- clearance channels.

As most small retailers will want a store presence I've also included some insights into a new-store opening checklist and how to project plan for a successful opening. This is a tried and tested model, based on working with Sarah Decent to open a new Modish outlet in Cambridge in 2011.

Tying into points raised in the previous chapters, Steps 4 and 5, we'll explore the possibility of having different ranges for the different channels – looking at extended ranges by mail order or e-commerce, for example – as well as separating off your clearance items to a specific clearance channel.

Finally we'll discuss the impact of multiple channels on the total customer journey and experience, the considerations you need to make in order to effectively embed multi-channel. I'll ask you to complete an assessment of what channels you *must* have to support your customers' expectations and what you *might* have to extend your reach and complement their experience.

At the end of this chapter you should be able to clearly document your channel strategy. You'll also have created a prioritized plan in order to develop your retail operations, to enable you to deliver on your customer promises, and to provide the service levels your customer expects. We'll be taking a look at how realistic your plan is, and if you believe you can't deliver the right level of service through a particular channel you should be putting that channel on hold until you can. Better to get it right than to alienate your customers.

So, without further ado, let's take a look at why multi-channel is relevant to a smaller, independent retail business and what multi-channel really means.

Why is multi-channel relevant to my retail business?

It has been proven that retailers who offer a truly integrated multi-channel experience secure greater loyalty from their customer base and that their cross-channel customers, on average, spend more.

A shop is only one part of the retailing equation. In this day and age you have no excuse not to also be selling online. In fact some well-known, successful retail brands started out online and then expanded into shops – think of The White Company and Hotel Chocolat. Both of these owner-run, entrepreneurial start-ups launched online before making the commitment to go into physical stores. Now their customer enjoys the benefit of being able to shop with them in-store, online, and via phone or mail order from their catalogues.

So you see it isn't just about shops vs online, either! The more creative you are with your channel strategy the more chances you have of 'being where your customers are'. Ask yourself, would your ideal customer buy from a catalogue or magazine? Would they buy from an at-home party-style occasion? Would they buy from fairs, fetes and festivals? The whole point of multi-channel is about widening the net, making sure that you balance the product presented with the channel and location, and offer a consistent service delivery (in line with your positioning) regardless of channel. It's fair to say, of your entire offer, what customers will buy in-store is different from what they might buy online, and different again from what they might buy from an at-home party-style occasion. We'll look at this in more detail towards the end of this chapter.

As a smaller retail business you need to be certain about the reason for adding channels to your business. We'll look at an interesting case study from Jacqueline Gold, CEO of Ann Summers, talking about when she first had the idea to launch 'Ann Summers Parties'.

It is good practice, and good sense, to analyse each channel uniquely to determine if and when you should add it to your business. You should speak to your loyal customers too; find out if they would welcome the opportunity to purchase from you through other channels, and if so, which? Would your customers enjoy receiving a catalogue from you to inform them about your range? Would they then buy from the catalogue, prefer to go online, or want to purchase in-store? When a customer understands that you share your information through different media and offer different options for transacting they like to mix them up! Think about your behaviours as a consumer – you might research online, visit a store, see the product physically, return home and finally buy online. In this way the channels support each other, the store played a role but the transaction took place through the online channel.

So a word of caution. While you really do need to understand the viability and business case for launching an additional channel, and you do need to monitor the performance of each channel as if it were a 'discrete' business, you also need to understand inter-channel relationships. Yes, of course you should analyse channel performance so that you understand the operating cost, the sales achieved and thus the profitability, but you also need to recognize that there is cross-over between channels that is highly complementary. It has been reported by various analysts in numerous different studies that a multi-channel customer is worth c. 130 per cent of the sales value of the same customer if only a single channel is offered. That's the crux of multi-channel – enabling a customer to interact with your business across channels. If you only ever looked at each channel in isolation you may feel, let's say, that the store is underperforming compared to online. However, you really need to understand the overall business performance, and the customer journey, before you decide to close the shop and just retail online. You may have missed that a key step in your customer's decision process was a visit to the store. You may attribute all the growth to online, but in fact the store's role as a 'showroom', a place for a customer to learn more about the product, has been critical to the sales process overall. It's just one to watch out for.

The concept of 'multi-channel' has been on the retailers' agenda for over a decade, since the early 2000s when transaction online was becoming possible and more acceptable to consumers. Of course multi-channel retailing has been around for many decades before that (albeit without online), but it's really only since the retail community has had access to technology to analyse customer behaviour (CRM systems, etc) that multi-channel as a concept, and as a total customer experience, was understood.

Consumers value the ability to access information from a retailer, and to transact with them, the way *they* want. Consumers increasingly expect more from retailers; we all have busy lives. If retailers can make it easier for us, as consumers, to buy from them the way we prefer, then we will stay loyal. As a smaller retailer, with the ambition to grow, you need to ensure that you are offering your customers access to buy from you in the way they want. If you don't they'll go elsewhere.

So multi-channel is all about offering access to your retail brand through many entry points. In addition it's about offering access to both information on products, pricing and promotions *and* the ability to buy from you through many transaction points. That is profoundly different from simply having multiple linear channels where a customer enters and progresses through to transaction in a single 'place'. If you really want to compete and grow it is essential to develop this multi-channel proposition and not just a series of independent channels. Let's look at what that *really* means, and the implications, in a bit more detail.

What does multi-channel retailing really mean?

When I say 'What does it mean?' I am not looking for a dictionary definition – I am thinking about what this means to your customer experience, your customer journey and to your retail operations.

It's really important, right from the outset, that you think about the implications of your ultimate multi-channel aims – they have far-reaching implications. Anyone can set up a transactional e-commerce site but you need to work through the customer experience, step by step, considering not only selling but also fulfilment. How will you get the goods to them? If they are dissatisfied how will you handle complaints and returns from remote customers? Are you aware of the different legislative requirements for selling to remote customers? All of this needs to be considered.

You can't afford not to consider every possibility because it will affect your customers' experience with you and their loyalty to you if you fail to meet the service proposition – the implied promises you make in your positioning. In recent years, developments in technology have meant that companies of all sizes have more ways of communicating with and transacting with their customers than ever before. If done correctly, multi-channel retailing can promote customer loyalty and drive increased sales – you'll be onto a winner. Get it wrong and there is a danger that confused or disappointing service could alienate customers and prompt them to turn to competitors. In a world fuelled by social media they may also tell their social network, their friends and connections, about their bad experience with you – not a good situation to find yourself in. That's why you really need to drill into the detail and be certain you can meet customer expectations before you offer any additional channels.

That said, don't hang about for long! Retailers who don't offer a truly integrated multi-channel experience will miss out – the research into cross-channel shoppers being of greatest value proves this. Consumers enjoy the flexibility of multi-channel and will dedicate more of their 'share of wallet' to those retailers who offer them a comprehensive cross-channel shopping experience. **In a time-poor, information-rich, online social world there is no excuse for every retailer, from single-store independents to major multi-nationals *not* to offer a multi-channel service experience.** This is the new norm; customers expect it and are quite taken aback when retailers are unable to provide it!

You need to be thinking multi-channel. While there is obviously an entry cost to launching a new channel I don't think any serious business can afford not to plan for it. You have to be where your customers, and potential customers, are. This is a concept we'll follow through into the next chapter, Step 7, customer engagement.

So, what investment is necessary to 'be' multi-channel?

This is a very wide area, and of course it will depend on what infrastructure you already have in place, what channels you plan to launch, and what service proposition you intend to offer.

You will need to consider the channels and the service proposition first before you can identify the 'ingredients' you will need in place to actually deliver the end-to-end customer experience.

Some of the things you should be considering are:

- Logistics infrastructure – where product is stored, picked, packed and shipped from when servicing remote customers. We'll talk a bit more about this in Step 8, supply chain.

- Contact centre – who will your '24/7 customer' call when you're not in the office? Who will answer questions, take enquiries, update on order status or handle complaints? You'll need to look at this in detail, as a professional retailer would provide their customer with access to a 24/7 contact centre.

- Systems infrastructure – from EPOS in-store to e-commerce online, from CRM and loyalty systems, to payment gateways and stock management. Technology will enable you both to sell product remotely and to be more effective in managing your total customer experience. We'll talk more about this in the IT part of Step 10, back office.

- Resource and training – if you are planning to roll out a party plan, for example, you would need to think about the deployment of people, in the field, to deliver a consistent brand experience. You need to think about how you will recruit, contract, train, reward and monitor those people. On the face of it an army of self-employed commission-only salespeople sounds brilliant – but like anything else it needs detailed consideration and management.

This is far from an exhaustive list; you would need to build up a list relevant to *your* business.

Putting all of that aside, the most important requirement in a world where consumers can spread news of their good and bad retail experiences to literally millions of others within minutes using social media is service. I would advise you to invest most effort in ensuring that your service promise is clearly expressed at every touchpoint with the customer. Make sure that through all your communication media your customer understands what to expect from you in terms of service experience. The investment in articulating your message will remove the risk of complaints about poor service, which typically have more to do with the retailer not managing the consumer's expectations than about the retailer failing to deliver on their promises. We'll look at this in more detail in the last part of this chapter.

Be where your customers are

This is a bit of a mantra for me; and it should be for you too. It's rather obvious when you say it, yet so many people are surprised by the concept. You want to make sure that you're not just overwhelmed by footfall, website traffic or phone enquiries that exhaust all of your resources but don't convert to sales; you want to make sure you're getting the right kind of traffic. We'll explore this with an example in Step 7 – because attracting the right kind of customers is part of the overall customer engagement piece.

Of course, as with many of the 10 steps to retail success, they are heavily interrelated: learnings from one step informing another.

Being where your customers are requires you to think back to Step 3 – ideal customer – you know the customer so well, like an imaginary friend. So where do they go? How do they shop? What do they want?

I'll give you an example. I have a client launching a menswear brand – he's designing, producing and then retailing his own range of products. He's done his research – if he wants to engage the guys who will actually wear his clothes he needs to market to them with a fun, relevant online TV channel.

His customers don't read magazines. If he were developing ladies wear it would be completely different. He needs to be where his customers are, and that's watching TV or surfing the net, not reading fashion magazines!

Knowing your customer will enable you to identify where you need to place yourself in terms of which channels, and when you are thinking about stores, which local areas – which towns, streets and positions are ideal for your stores based on your customers' expectations.

In the next part we'll review the channel options, then there is an exercise for you to complete that will get you thinking about which are right for your business and your customer.

What are the options?

As listed in the introduction, there are numerous possibilities, not all of which would be relevant to all retailers. I'm going to give an overview on those channels that are the most commonly used – this won't be all the possibilities but should give you a flavour of some popular options so you can consider which should be a part of your channel and location strategy. The ones I'll talk a bit more about include:

- stores (including market stalls and concessions);
- e-commerce (including mobile and apps);
- party plans;
- consumer events (fetes and fairs, occasional markets and shows);
- catalogues: mail order/phone order;
- clearance channels.

Stores

By stores I actually mean, in generic terms, permanent physical outlets where you will regularly be found by your customer. I include market stalls as you may have a regular pitch; perhaps not daily, but it is still regular. I consider that to be different from an event market such as a craft fair, a county show or a Christmas market – that's obviously occasion based.

I also include concessions – although these aren't your own outlet they are still your store within a store, they carry your stock, serve your customer and usually are staffed by your people.

Essentially what we are looking at here are permanent physical locations that offer the consumer the chance to see your product, purchase it, and take it away with them.

Physicality of location (this can include stores, parties and events) is a key feature. These are the only channels where customers can actually touch the merchandise before transacting, and in the most part (except for products only available by special order) consumers can also take their purchases away with them, there and then, from physical locations. Stores are the permanent physical locations; parties and events are occasion based and non-permanent, but they are still physical and share some of the same benefits and drawbacks.

Physical retailing benefits from the convenience of immediate fulfilment, often referred to as 'instant gratification'. The drawback that comes hand-in-hand with this is of course the overhead of having to carry stock in multiple locations. When it comes to remote channels, while unable to offer instant gratification, they do benefit from the fact that stock for *all* remote transaction points (e-commerce, mail order, phone order) can be held at a central location. This is something worth bearing in mind as it does impact on the cost of stock you need to carry in each channel, so touches on both supply chain (Step 8) and planning and controlling (Step 9).

In order to make the most of your permanent physical locations, your stores, stalls or concessions, you need to develop a detailed location plan. You need to identify not only the towns or shopping malls where you should locate your shops or future shops, but also who your neighbours will be and what size of shop would ideally suit you. As with the product, you need to make sure your locations are exactly where your customers would want to go.

If you are thinking of opening your first store it obviously makes most sense to open in a location that is easy for you to get to – you'll have enough on your plate opening a new outlet without adding a long commute to your workload!

If you already have a store and want to expand, do consider what is good and bad about your current location and set-up; what you would change, what you would keep. Bear that 'shopping list' in mind when identifying your next outlet. And, to quote Hussein Lalani, co-founder of 99p Stores:

> With any successful retail venture you perfect the model with the first few stores, developing an ideal store, and once you've get it perfected it's just a case of replicating it and rolling it out.

Essentially what Hussein is saying is that you should develop a 'robust and repeatable model'. He knows what he is talking about. He started 99p with a single store. Within 10 years he went from start-up to 150 stores. He now plans a further 150 stores in just four more years!

Next, consider the towns and shopping centres that might meet your ideal requirements – visit the places you feel might be right for you, have a good look around, speak to shop owners and customers if you can. Do your research. If you find a unit available that you think would suit you then make sure you negotiate well on your lease – investing in a specialist retail lawyer to work on your lease on your behalf will protect you from unexpected costs and save you their professional services fee many times over during the life of the lease.

Finally, when it comes to opening, you need a project plan, with deadlines and due dates, and you need to keep on top of all suppliers, service providers – everyone – because if one party misses a date you might end up delaying your opening, meaning that you're paying your rent but not making any sales!

Below is a list, a rough guide to some of the things you need to think about when opening a new store:

- Ordering your phone line, broadband and setting up your wi-fi. More often than not this is actually the part of the process that holds up opening as EPOS often can't function without broadband, or the credit card machine won't operate without a phone line. Countless retailers, start-ups, medium and large, have been caught out by the length of time this can take – so get it ordered as soon as you know you have secured the lease.

- Staff: recruitment and training. You're allowed to advertise for staff before you've secured the lease – you don't have to make any job offers until you know you're opening. I'd advise you to involve the support of a third-party HR expert who can help you with interviewing, contracts and general employment policies. When it comes to training you might be able to get a bit creative – can you get someone to film certain processes, such as serving a customer, so you can show a video as part of training? Mostly, training will be on the job, things like where to find stock, how to use the till, cash handling, use of the credit card machine, etc. As you train your staff for your opening try to keep a note of what you cover, or sound record what you say; that way you can get your conversations audio typed, and with a bit of editing you'll have the basis for a training guide for next time.

- Flooring, lighting, decor, fixtures, merchandising elements. If the shop needs a refit you need a clear timeline from the contractor as to exactly when you could merchandise (add product, window dressing, etc) the store ready for opening.

- Signage, frontage, window. You might need the support of a design agency to get this done for you. Don't forget your shop front is your advertisement to passers-by, so it's well worth spending a reasonable amount to make sure you get a good result.

- Carrier bags, business cards/compliments slips. Again you might need a design agency to look at this – they may also be able to find you a good printer to produce the materials.

- Website update. Let people know about your new opening via your website, your blog, Facebook, Twitter – everywhere you can. Trickle-feed news/info/opening offers/launch party dates, etc to keep their interest.

- STOCK. Quite important! Make sure you've placed your orders for any stock you need and have a clear delivery schedule from your suppliers so you know what is arriving, and when.

- Stock room fit-out. How you keep your stock is important to how quickly you can replenish, fetch items for a customer, and also to making sure the stock is in tip-top condition. Don't forget to plan the stock room – it's a regular omission with all the attention being on the shop floor and suddenly stock arrives and you have nowhere to put it!

- PR, local marketing, launch event, press release, leaflet drop, radio ads. You need a marketing plan to announce your launch – be creative! Try and get the support of a local PR agency for the launch; it should pay back in terms of hitting the ground running when it comes to sales.

- Utilities – water, gas, electric, heating system, etc. Make sure these are safe and tested; ideally get the landlord to take responsibility in the assigning of the lease. Then you need to remember to take over the accounts for these.

- Consumables. In addition to your carrier bags you'll need office items such as pens, sticky tape, stapler, etc. Make sure you get all of these items – it can be very frustrating when you can't find a pen!

- Office/staffroom. You need to provision for a space for staff to take a break and for some admin to be done (eg cashing up, preparing the banking).

- Back rooms – kitchenette, toilets. You need to make sure that there are adequate and usable toilets, in line with regulations, and also if you are providing 'comfort' facilities for staff, such as tea and coffee making, that you have provisioned suitable equipment.

- Fire escapes, evacuation process, H&S, etc. You need to check what should be in place for your type of outlet in order to be compliant with all fire, health and safety regulations.

- Notify authorities. In some areas you need to notify postal services, local council and local police about the change of business at a commercial address.

- Check for security systems. Are a security system and smoke detection in place? If so, they should be tested. If they ring through to a monitoring station you will need to give them your contact details in case of an emergency.

- Till system. Depending on what you are planning to use you may well need computers, printers, credit card machine, cash drawer and anything else as specified by the provider if you are using EPOS.

Etc, etc, etc!

So opening a shop is not for the faint-hearted! If you've not yet run for the hills and are still thinking of opening a new store, you should create a store-opening checklist, like the one below. It could be a really handy guide.

TABLE 6.1   Store opening checklist template

Activity	Dependent actions	Deadline date	Lead time	Status
Installing phone line and broadband	Confirming contract with supplier, agreeing install dates	Three days before opening to test till system and card machine	Allow 20 working days from confirming contract	Make any notes here as to what has been done, eg contract confirmed on [date], install date booked for [date]
Setting up till system and credit card machine	Phone lines and broadband are functional	Three days before opening in order to be ready for pre-opening staff training	Allow half a day to set up; can be done as soon as telecoms are live	
Staff: recruitment	Contracts signed four weeks before opening			
Staff: training	Training on days one and two before opening (depends on access to till system and phone/broadband being live)			

To give you a head start, a template based on the table and populated with a list of things to consider is available for download in the resources area **www.retailchampion.co.uk/resources** – it's called 'template store opening checklist'. It is in Excel so you can add your own ideas to it and use filters and sort functions to review items by due date, etc. If you're a real whizz on a PC you could create a store-opening project plan using a tool like Microsoft Project. Each activity can be shown as part of a timeline in Gantt chart format. Activities can be linked where there are dependencies in order to identify your critical path/critical dates. MS Project is brilliant, if you can use it. If not, Excel will be good enough. In terms of what it could look like, some ideas are in the table, I've filled in the top two rows by way of example.

You would complete your list, based on the bullet points as well as anything else that might be relevant to you.

So stores are important. Stores allow the consumer the opportunity to interact with a product, to sample it, to speak to a sales advisor and to browse other associated items. Even if a consumer decides to transact their purchase online, the store will have been instrumental in the purchase decision. While many successful retailers started out as 'pure play' retailers (online only) the majority added stores as soon as they had the cash in the business to do so. For most retailers having a permanent physical presence is fundamental to their strategy.

As multi-channel retailing has evolved, stores have added value to the multi-channel service proposition – providing a stocking location from which the retailer can fulfil orders and prepare items for the customer to collect.

I could probably write a couple more chapters on all the considerations for store opening alone, but we need to complete all 10 steps to retail success; so let's move on to the next channel.

E-commerce

E-commerce is the ability to sell products via a transactional website. This also expands into mobile websites (sometimes termed m-commerce) and 'apps'.

An 'app' is short for an application; a programme that would usually be downloaded to a smartphone or other device with mobile internet access. Apps can only be used once someone has taken the time to download them. A mobile website is a version of a normal website that is adapted to the smaller screen and touch interface that would be typical on a smartphone. It can be used instantly from a mobile browser. Apps and mobile websites are very different.

E-commerce is common sense when you think about it. Essentially the website has to replace the activities that a store environment can deliver. It has to present the product and provide information about it. It has to perform the role of a sales assistant with such features as 'Click here for more details', up-sell and cross-sell, eg 'Other customers who bought item X also bought item Y'. It has to provide easy 'flow' around the site for the customer, using navigation via menus and filters – exactly the same thinking and objectives as store layout and visual merchandising.

Often, smaller retailers need to add more 'visual-merchandising' thinking to their transactional websites. A good e-commerce site can exceed the rates of sale that your best store could ever achieve. All too often smaller retailers invest a minimal budget in the aesthetics and navigation of a website. Equally limited funds are spent on the website 'sales assistant' – that is the key product information and images that enable the customer to buy with confidence.

You need to realize that a bad website could damage your brand and negatively influence your customers' perception of your business – it is all back to positioning again. When it comes to design and development of your website I would advise that you allocate a budget similar to what you would spend on a store refit. Then you need to allow ongoing budget for the maintenance of the site – adding new products, new images, updating pricing and promotions – as well as the ongoing internet marketing to drive traffic to the site. In the same way that a store needs full-time sales resources so does the website! You should allocate funds equivalent to the cost of an FTE to buy in the services of an internet marketing business to manage, maintain, optimize and market your e-commerce site. If you don't put the effort in you'll not get the results – it's as simple as that.

E-commerce doesn't require premises to sell, but does need resources to serve. When setting up e-commerce you need to consider that many customers prefer to make a phone order – so a third-party call centre, ideally with 24/7 opening hours, who can take enquiries, orders, payment, provide updates on orders already in the system, and record complaints, is incredibly important. There are companies who offer this as a standard service – virtual call handling for e-commerce – if you do some research you'd be surprised what good value their services can be: often charged per call/ enquiry. One thing is certain, if using a call centre makes the difference between getting a transaction or not, they'll soon pay back your investment in their service.

The other resource to serve e-commerce customers that you will need in place is a fulfilment operation. Many smaller retailers start out doing pick, pack and despatch from their home. It's one way of doing it, but it's not ideal. If you want to compete with the big players you need a quality operation, not one at risk of failure due to being run on a shoestring. It is surprising how affordable third-party fulfilment providers can be – do your research and then select a right provider that matches your service proposition – and make sure they can also handle returns!

Consider these services – call centre and fulfilment operations – as overheads of running your e-commerce channel. You need to account for these costs in order to understand the profitability of your e-commerce.

E-commerce should still be a lower-cost channel that delivers very good sales performance. If you don't cut corners but work with experts in each aspect – design, build, internet marketing, customer care and order fulfilment – you should have an e-commerce presence that rivals the big retailers in the eyes of the customer; and one that achieves a great contribution to your bottom line.

E-commerce and stores are typically the only two channels that smaller retailers consider. So, let's now look at some of the other channels, some a bit 'unusual' for smaller retailers, but there is no reason why you shouldn't include these channels if that's what your customer would welcome.

Party plans

Tupperware and Ann Summers are the well-known names in the at-home party retail market. Recently many, many more have come to market – The Body Shop, Silpada (Jewellery), Jamie At Home (Jamie Oliver branded cookware), Pampered Chef and Phoenix Cards, to name a handful from the UK.

Party plans usually engage a commission-only agent to sell their products. The agent often invests in the stock and is given training on how to sell the product effectively. Then it's up to the agent to make it work.

This type of retailing is ideally suited if you design and produce your own products – if you are retailing branded products purchased from a supplier it is less relevant.

Parties take advantage of the social network of the agent. Success depends on their ability to gather a group of friends at a party host's home and to make the occasion as much a fun, social event as it is an opportunity to sell. For some brands the parties are more of an introduction to the product, an opportunity to try them out in a fun environment. For other brands this is their only route to market.

Before diving into this channel I suggest you go along to some party events for other brands, as a guest, to see what it's all about. Speak to the agents to find out what the brand does for them, how they are contracted, trained and rewarded. This kind of research will be invaluable to you as you shape your ideas and think about how you could set up a party plan of your own.

If you think this is a channel that could work for you then test the concept by attempting to run a few parties yourself first (or inviting your staff to do so). If you find that your ranges work well in a party-retail environment then a few trial events will help you to refine the process that works best for your brand. Of course trials may prove it's not a channel for you.

Let me give you an example of a brand it really does work for.

Ann Summers in the UK is a multi-channel lingerie and adult-products re-tailer. Today they have a strong high street presence, but it wasn't always that way. Ann Summers is owned by Gold Group International, which is headed up by David Gold, Jacqueline Gold's father. Jacqueline became CEO in 1993 having joined the business as a payroll clerk in 1977, with no long-term plans to stay. However, Jacqueline saw an opportunity to break down some of the taboos, give women a new and exciting retail experience, and to grow and diversify the business. Here is her story, about how Ann Summers started out with party plan:

> Building Ann Summers to the business it is today has definitely given me some challenges over the years! When I first started work at Ann Summers I didn't plan to stay, however I spotted an opportunity to make Ann Summers a brand that offered something totally unique and I had to make that happen.
>
> I remember the initial pitch I made to the board in which I pitched my party plan concept. I came up against a level of resistance with one board member even telling me that women didn't even like sex so why would they be interested in this idea!! I think that said more about his sex life than it did about my idea! I'm pleased to say though that the board did eventually say yes and party plan was born and an instant success.
>
> In the early days I had to overcome a lot of hurdles, however I always had great feedback from the women who attended parties so I knew that the business was going to continue to be a success. Once party plan was established, I saw that there was a real opportunity to launch Ann Summers as a retail concept and this was a time when I experienced most resistance. This resistance was mainly from councils and men who were for some reason threatened by what Ann Summers stood for. From bullets through the post and a couple of arrests, I'm pleased to say that I am still standing and that Ann Summers is absolutely thriving!
>
> Breaking in to the high street was for me the time when perceptions of Ann Summers and its offering really started to change. People saw that Ann Summers wasn't a back street, blacked out windows sex-store and was instead part of the British High Street.
>
> The feedback we have from customers every day of the week proves to me that Ann Summers is as unique and in demand as it was when I started over 30 years ago.

I like this story because it just goes to show that even those big, successful retailers started somewhere! Ann Summers is probably *the* leader in party-based retailing in the UK today, the model a small business might aspire to. Knowing that it might never have happened without Jacqueline's determination should be some comfort to any smaller retailer with *big* plans!

So, that's as much as I have to share regarding party plans – you'll know if this channel is likely to work for you or not.

Consumer events: fetes, fairs and events

Occasional events are a good way to increase sales, if you've got the stock and resources to do it. However, these events can often charge a considerable sum for a stall or stand. One of my clients told me she had spent over £4,500 for a small stand in the 'Ideal Shopping' area at the Ideal Home show; and got almost nothing back for it.

You should consider the events most relevant to your customer, analyse the total cost of getting involved (stall fee, staff time, transport, merchandising, any accommodation costs, etc), and work out if you are likely to make sufficient margin on sales to cover the costs. If it looks marginal then it is probably not worth it – it's too risky.

Catalogues, mail order

If you are already running an e-commerce proposition then it's very straightforward to provide a catalogue alongside it. You'll already have the infrastructure for handling calls and issuing orders.

There is a lot of cost, however – design and print of the catalogue, postage to your database – and if you don't get any incremental sales it is wasted investment.

The other risk with catalogues is that you have no flexibility in pricing – once they are printed you have 'published' your pricing. It's not dynamic like your website would be.

Lots of retailers these days are publishing small A5 booklets rather than bigger catalogues. These are like promotional flyers, driving traffic to the store or the e-commerce site. They are magazine-style publications, with editorial about product as well as the classic content of product images and descriptions.

I am sure by now you know what I'm going to say – think about your ideal customer. Would they browse a catalogue that was sent by post, or would it go straight into the recycling bin? Would they prefer just an e-mail from you to inform them of special offers and direct them to your website/ invite them into your store? As with all the other channels think it through carefully before you waste a lot of money producing a catalogue that delivers no additional sales.

Clearance channels

These are usually dedicated channels that are recognized by consumers as offering clearance products from retailers and manufactures. Consumers expect big discounts *but* are usually not just browsing, they're buying! They are unlikely to be your ideal customer; this is the domain of a real bargain hunter!

Clearance online can be done via Amazon Marketplace and eBay shops – this option takes advantage of the vast amount of traffic these websites get. Clearance can also be done through a store, typically in a mall or area dedicated to 'outlets' (the clearance channel associated with a major brand). The only issue here is that you've got to have a great deal of volume coming through in order to make enough margin to cover your rent. If you're only generating clearance from a small initial order quantity you'll never have enough residual product to supply a high-turnover outlet. For most smaller retailers eBay and Amazon are the ideal place for a clearance channel.

Next we'll use some of these thoughts to consider which channels you ideally should be planning for in your business.

Appraising the ideal channels for your business and your ideal customer

As mentioned earlier, this exercise is for you to get thinking about how each channel could work for *your* ideal customer. You should complete the grid overleaf, or you can download one from the resources area **www.retailchampion.co.uk/resources** – it's called 'template channel analysis'. This should help to kick-start your thinking about which channels would be most relevant to you. On the grid overleaf I've done the first row by way of example.

This exercise will not only help you to work through which channels are most relevant to you, but will also help you to consider each channel through the eyes of your ideal customer. When you have worked through the reasons why the customer would want the channel you can prioritize the channel accordingly in your development plans. This channel analysis could also be used to support the narrative in your business plan, if you intend to use your business plan to secure funding for growth from a bank or investor.

One final thing to consider, before we look at the logistical implications of multi-channel in more detail, is the assortment. Will you have the same assortment offered through all channels/stores? Will you offer a different choice of products to customers of different channels?

TABLE 6.2 Channel analysis template

Channel	Relevance to ideal customer	Reason	Priority	Strategy/aim
Store(s)	Expected, needed	Interaction with product, helpful staff	Top priority, primary channel	Increase store numbers – target five new stores in three years; focus on sites of c. 500 sq ft in middle-class market towns. Position as close to main high street/marketplace as possible *or* any focal points such as small mall/shopping centre
E-commerce	...	...	...	
Mobile transactional site/app				
Party plan				
Consumer events				
Catalogue/ mail order				
Clearance channel				

Channel-specific ranges?

In both Steps 4 and 5 I touched briefly on the idea of channel-specific or store-specific product assortments. This is a decision for you, the business owner. Do you want customers to be able to purchase any of your products from any store or channel? Perhaps if you are tight on store space you would want to offer an extended range through other channels? You might even offer variations in the assortment presented at different stores – to take advantage of the more specific needs and wants of the local catchment area.

There isn't a right or wrong answer for this; as ever it links back to your mission, positioning and ideal customer – you should ask yourself: What fits best with those guiding principles of your business?

Obviously there is a management overhead with extending ranges. These include:

- buying: more products to select, price and stock-manage;
- stock: more stockholding as minimum order quantities are needed on everything you buy;
- logistics: more complexity in allocating stock to stores/channels due to not all items being sold from all locations/channels;
- productivity: high risk of obsolescence as you've potentially shared demand between more products and not channelled the same volume of demand through fewer products;
- customer: risk of alienating customers if they can see an item available through one channel and yet can't purchase it through another.

So my honest advice for a smaller business is to avoid varying the assortment by location or channel unless you feel it is absolutely necessary and what your customer expects.

There is an occasion where a different range would make sense, however: clearance channels. If you're positioned at the upper end in your market you should be avoiding heavy discounting – as we covered in the previous chapter. If you run a clearance channel through websites like eBay and Amazon Marketplace you can completely separate your full-price merchandise from your major reductions. The main purpose of clearance channels is to avoid devaluing your brand or product, and to avoid diverting your full-price customer into low-margin, clearance items by having that separation.

Having now considered all the different channel options and variable ranges by channel, the final part of this chapter will be about the impact of multiple channels on the total customer journey and experience, the considerations you need to make in order to effectively embed multi-channel into your retail operations.

Assessing operational impact on addition of channels

By now you'll realize that **it is no longer an option for retailers to offer a seamless buying experience through multiple channels; it's essential.**

Achieving it doesn't have to be costly, but it does have to be well thought out, not just from a front-end point of view, but also in terms of the total fulfilment chain and the service promises the retail brand is willing to make to the customer.

Many retailers I speak to are surprised at how cost effective third-party storage with pick, pack and despatch can be – certainly if you cost the ongoing maintenance of an e-commerce website and the operational infrastructure to support customer orders you'll be surprised how favourably it can look compared to leasing a shop. That said, you do need to have a comprehensive internet marketing strategy that includes search marketing and social media marketing in order to ensure you get sufficient of the right kind of traffic to the website to achieve a rate of sale comparable to your stores. We'll look at this in the next chapter when we talk about attracting customers.

What do you need to put in place?

Taking the list of channels you'd want to implement (based on the grid you completed earlier), you now need to think about the 'ingredients' that will need to be in place in order for you to deliver your end-to-end customer experience for all the channels you plan to adopt.

Create a list of what's required and work this through in order to create your action plan. I've done one example to bring this to life and added a few ideas that will help you work it through. You can also download this template from **www.retailchampion.co.uk/resources** – it's called 'template multi-channel operational action plan'.

Using this you should now have a fairly good idea about what channels you want to develop into and what operational activities will be required in order to meet your customer promise.

I hope you are feeling very positive about building a relevant, well-positioned multi-channel retail empire. I am sure it's also a little daunting, but having completed the exercises above, and broken the strategy down into a series of prioritized actions, with due dates, you should feel more 'in control'. The outcome of the exercise will provide you with a much more manageable and achievable action plan as well as clarity about what needs to be in place before you 'switch on' a channel. You can take it at your own pace – the key is to have a plan, to make sure it is realistic, and not to launch a new channel without having tested every step of the customer journey first. If you believe that you can't deliver the expected level of service through

TABLE 6.3 Multi-channel operational action plan template

What's required?	Why? What does it support?	How important is it? (Does it support more than 1 channel, etc?)	When? What is your time frame on this, when does it need to be in place?	Cost – what is the expenditure required to enable this?
Third-party pick, pack and despatch operation	All non-store-based fulfilment	Very high priority – enables several channels	Must be in place before e-commerce launch	Initially a couple of days to research the options, brief possible suppliers and analyse quotes. Will not know full costs until all quotes are received and compared back to requirements.
Returns policy	To communicate what the process is for returns, when refunds would be given, how to make a return, etc			
Remote selling – legislative compliance	To remain compliant with the law, to protect the business and the consumer			
Payment gateway	To take credit card payments online			
Third-party call centre	To manage enquiries from remote customers as to order status, complaints, etc			

a particular channel then you should be putting that channel on hold until you can. Better to get it right than to alienate your customers.

Summing up

Congratulations for completing Step 6, channel and location.

In this chapter we have looked at the meaning of multi-channel retailing, why it is important and why it is relevant to a smaller (but growing) retail business.

We talked about the importance of 'being where your customers are' and talked about the most popular channels in terms of options that could be available to you. Then we looked at each of those channels in the context of how those possible options could relate to your future multi-channel proposition. We worked through an exercise to determine which of these sales channels would be most relevant to your business and your customer, including an element of consideration for your strategy and reasons why.

We spent a moment just reflecting on the possibility of having different ranges and different assortments presented to your customers through different channels, tying in with some of the thoughts from Steps 4 and 5.

Finally we've taken a good look at what multi-channel means to *your* total customer journey and completed an assessment of what you need to have in place before you launch a channel in order to deliver on your customer promises.

You should now have everything you need to be able to clearly document your channel strategy. You'll also have a prioritized plan in order to develop your retail operations to enable you to deliver on your customer promises and to provide the service levels your customer expects.

Multi-channel retailing is the way forward, enabling you to increase customer loyalty and sales. In modern retailing it is expected, so if you are serious about developing a scalable, saleable retail enterprise you'll need to make sure you are a genuine multi-channel retailer.

So, now you've extended your reach and made yourself accessible to your ideal customer, you need to attract, convert and retain them and get them recommending you to their friends! Well, that's where the next step comes in; Step 7, customer engagement.

Step Seven
Customer engagement

Introduction

Welcome to Step 7 – customer engagement. This is one step where a smaller retailer can really make their mark. It's not an area which can be done that much better due to better systems, better technology or availability of finance. In this step you are able to compete on a level playing field with the major chains – so there are no excuses for *not* getting this absolutely right.

In this chapter we'll take a look once again at 'being where your customers are' – but unlike the perspective we took in the last step on multi-channel, this is about being where they are in the context of your brand visibility and findability. In this section we'll highlight the importance of the internet, even if you don't yet sell online.

Next, I'll walk through how I distil the whole concept of customer engagement into four actions, which are cyclical, not linear. This cyclical approach, when undertaken effectively, can create a self-sustaining upward spiral. At the same time however, if done badly, it can have the reverse effect.

These actions are:

1 Attraction
2 Conversion
3 Retention
4 Recommendation.

The first three of which are entirely up to *you* as the retailer; the fourth you can encourage but is down to your customer. Success in the fourth action is really the result of you having been successful in actions one to three.

Through this chapter I'll be asking you to think about the following questions:

- Do you know what attracted your existing customers?
- Do you measure customer conversion rates through each of your channels?
- Do you have a process to increase customer retention and reward loyalty?

- Do you encourage happy customers to recommend your business to others?

The honest answers should be used to create aspects of your action plan.

At the end of this chapter you will better understand how to attract more of your ideal customer using relevant methods from traditional advertising and PR, to online marketing and social media. You'll be clear as to why it's important to measure conversions, and how to go about it. You'll have worked through ideas that will enable your business to increase customer retention and loyalty. Finally, you'll be conversant with methods to encourage advocacy within your loyal customer base, which in turn will increase your attractiveness to new customers, thus developing your upward spiral of customer engagement.

This chapter will be as important to your business as knowing what products to sell, for what price and through which channels. In fact, I'd go as far as to say you can get Steps 4, 5 and 6 perfected, but if you fail on Step 7 you'll have no business.

So, as this is the most important step to take you from concept to realization, let's get started!

Be where your customers are!

In the previous chapter we looked at the concept of 'being where your customers are' from the perspective of implementing channels that suited their purchasing preferences. Being multi-channel, and offering your products in a way that is convenient to your customers will increase customer acquisition and retention; we'll look at how later in this chapter. In this section we're going to reflect on 'being where your customers are' *before* they are your customers. We'll consider how to access potential customers by both increasing your visibility to them and, if they are looking for products or services that you offer, by increasing your findability as well.

It is no secret that consumers are online *a lot*. Access to the internet in the home, in the workplace, and on the move is now common, and expected, in many countries in the world. Findings show that the internet plays a very important role in consumers' lives. From researching products that might meet their needs and wants, reading reviews and finding stockists, to 'Googling' for 'Where can I buy camping equipment in [my town]?', to sharing experiences, reviews, recommendations and discount vouchers on social networks and social media. I am sure you can recognize some of the things you do online in that list.

Since consumers are so engaged by online social networks such as Facebook and in social media such as Twitter it is inexcusable for a serious business, of any size, not to have a presence.

Why are social media and online important?

Apart from an obvious high street presence, online is your biggest opportunity to be where your customers are (or where those who influence your customers are). When we look at 'attraction' we'll review the vast range of marketing and PR options. The majority of these come at a price. Most of the options online can be set up for free, apart from the time to put in place. Also, reflect on your life – are you busy? Are you overwhelmed with marketing messages on TV, billboards, flyers, radio, newspapers, etc? Do you pay attention to much of it?

Traditional advertising is 'shouting' at us constantly and incessantly *but* it has been proven that it is failing. Our ability to access the internet, find things out for ourselves and to speak to other people who use a product or service has shifted our attention away from the 'noise' and to a more focused, more personal interaction with content. This has enabled us to draw our own conclusions about what to buy and who to buy from, without as much influence from external advertising messages as there would have been in the past. Some commentators will say it is as a result of the global economic downturn; we have lost confidence in *big* brands making *big* promises. Their theory is that when several of the most trusted organizations (such as banks and insurance companies) collapsed, consumers suddenly felt very insecure about placing their trust with big brands. They turned to 'people just like them' for advice, people they could relate to and identify with more easily. Whatever the reason for this change there is no denying that there has been a powerful shift in the basis of trust away from 'corporate to consumer' and towards 'consumer to consumer'. Power of influence now resides in the peer group, the 'people just like me'. It has been termed 'word of mouth on steroids' – a humorous analogy, but actually rather accurate if you think about it in the context of how rapidly consumer review can be shared, thanks to the internet and social networks.

While it may be proven that traditional, offline media can work for your business, whether you like it or not, your customers and those who influence them *will* be turning to online resources to research products, services and reviews *before* they buy from you. They will be leaving online reviews and comments *after* they buy from you as well. This full-circle approach to your customer – considering their actions before, during and after transaction with you – will enable you to make the upward cycle work for you. Think about the customer engagement process with you as the total experience – before, during and after. Think about how your customer feels. Look at the example below – have you felt this way before?

- Attract – 'I've done my research online, I've found some good reviews... I trust this brand to be able to provide for my needs.'

- Convert – 'Their service proposition matches my expectations; the product I want is available; the price is fair... I will buy from this brand.'

- Retain – 'This brand values me. They have kept in communication with me; they cared about me as an individual and thanked me for spending some of my hard-earned cash with them. I will come back to this brand.'

- Recommend – 'I want to tell my network about this brand – I've had a good experience and I want to share that with others. I want people I know to enjoy a good experience too. I will recommend this brand.'

And the upward cycle is created. Although much of the attraction and subsequent recommendation could have been achieved through traditional conversations, the fact that online media make it more instant, more accessible to more people and more permanent should be evidence enough that online is one of the most important ingredients in retailing today... even if you don't have a transactional e-commerce site, yet!

Before we dig deeper into the four actions I want to share some thoughts about mobile, which is a very rapidly growing area and of increasing importance in many ways.

Importance of mobile

Let's take a moment to reflect on the importance of mobile. Globally the use of mobile devices is increasing; not just phones and smartphones but *any* portable device that enables the consumer to access the internet on the move.

Retailers of all sizes need to consider the relevance, now and in the coming years, of mobile to their ideal customer group.

In 2010 figures showed that the most popular use of smartphones specifically was to access social media, closely followed by search. By 2011 research findings indicated that 54 per cent of consumers in the UK would be comfortable shopping on a mobile. Other research highlighted there was a very strong trend towards using the smartphone while shopping – to research competitor pricing, to find more detailed product information than was available in-store, or to read product reviews before committing to the purchase. By 2011 sales of smartphones and tablet PCs were outstripping laptops and desktop PCs. We can safely conclude that within a very short time the consumer will be entirely 'mobilized'. Access to the internet via a laptop or desktop will soon be considered very outmoded, possibly only done in the workplace.

We can be confident that there is a preference towards mobile. That changes a few things. The convenience and immediacy of the content on the web are now in your pocket. They are also in the customers' pockets.

Retailers need to adapt to this behaviour. It's not just about ensuring your e-commerce design is mobile compatible, with a front end that can be interpreted and correctly displayed on a variety of devices and through a range of operating systems – that's merely scratching the surface!

Local search should be part of your mobile marketing strategy

Think about consumers who perhaps are in an unfamiliar area. They decide they have time for a bit of 'retail therapy' and will turn to their mobiles to search for what they want in the area where they currently are. Any retailer not considering how they can leverage location-based search as part of their 'attraction' processes could be missing out on a considerable amount of incremental sales and footfall. This has been proven to already be of huge value for clients of e-mphasis internet marketing (one of my other businesses) with the volume of traffic from mobile being the primary driver of growth in location-based search. Many retailers have assumed that online search will lead to online transactions. Not so; statistics suggest that over 60 per cent of consumers perform an internet search in advance of visiting a store to complete their purchase. If retailers embed a local angle to their internet marketing they'll be able to capitalize on a great deal of consumer search taking place on mobiles.

Other innovation fuelled by the increased use of mobile

It doesn't end there, either – mobiles can help you with customer acquisition, enable a transaction *and* can be a payment method! Have you heard of Google Wallet, for instance? This is just one of the increasing number of payment options available using a mobile as your payment method. Other emerging options include:

- using a text message to authorize a payment on your credit card;
- charging a purchase to a mobile phone bill or using mobile phone credit to pay for items in a shop;
- contactless – using proximity technology, pioneered by Barclaycard, that can be within a phone and used to authorize small transactions simply by 'touching' your mobile onto a reader.

And we'll probably see more innovation in the next few years along these lines.

Outside the attraction, transaction and payment uses of mobile, there are many other methods that retailers can use to take advantage of the ubiquitous nature of these devices. Using SMS messaging (which doesn't even require a smartphone), retailers can deliver marketing messages to customers, communicate deliveries are being shipped and share details of special offers. So many types of communication could be sent by SMS (text message) and yet this is still an underused approach.

That's really all I need to say on the topic of the importance of mobile. It's important. It's getting more important. Therefore in all your thinking about how to take your business forward, think about engaging your mobile customer too.

At that point we're ready to start to dig deeper into the four-step cycle. And we'll get started with an introduction to the concept.

Four-step cycle

This four-step cycle is one I developed to simplify the customer engagement process into four distinct stages. It's a cycle because each stage leads to the next, and, if you do it right, it leads to increasing levels of attraction thanks to past customer recommendation, as in the example I gave earlier.

Of course, it can work against you – and hence why until now we've built up all the ingredients that should ensure you won't fail. Your attraction will be deeply rooted in your mission, positioning and ideal customer. The conversion will be based on your product offer, pricing and promotions and channels offered to complete the transaction. There is without a doubt a necessity for stock availability to complete the conversion step – and that will be discussed in Steps 8 and 9, supply chain and planning. Retention is to do with your ability to offer a consistent level of service – to meet all the promises you made in the attraction and conversion steps. Consistency can only be achieved if you have robust, repeatable processes and systems – one of the overarching messages I am sharing with you in this book. Finally,

FIGURE 7.1   The four-step cycle of customer engagement

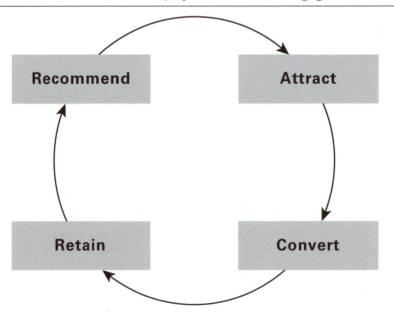

recommendation comes when you have retained the customer, proven you do offer consistency, you do deliver on your promises, and once they have come to trust you.

So, let's look at step 1 of the cycle – attraction.

Attract

This is about everything that we've covered to this point – your mission, your positioning, your customer, your product, your pricing and promotions, and your channels. It is all about having the right outward impact on the world to draw in those you want to target.

It's also about creating some noise – with PR, marketing and social media. These elements all add to the process of attraction. Fundamentally, it's about communicating what you've got to offer and why people should become your customer. So, how do you go about creating 'noise'?

Well, there are two ways to create some 'noise' to draw attention to your business:

1 You can make it yourself.

2 You get other people (partners, suppliers, happy customers, etc) to make it for you.

Before we drill into these points in more detail can you first honestly answer this question:

- Do you know what attracted your existing customers?

If you genuinely know the answer, then consider how you can apply that knowledge to attract more of the same. If you don't know the answer you need to find out; you need to ask them. Try to get some insight on this as it will help you focus your efforts in 'making noise' on the most appropriate methods and messaging.

So, let's now take a look at some of those methods.

'Noise' you can make yourself

Looking first at what you can do yourself, and this is by no means an exhaustive list, some of the options include:

- doing leaflet drops in the local area;
- running local newspaper advertisements – perhaps with special offers/coupons;
- approaching other retailers/local businesses and organizations who share a similar customer base and creating a co-promotion;
- advertising on local radio.

- getting involved in local campaigns, eg for small businesses, for retailers – taking an active role in community issues;
- making sure your search marketing is up to scratch – focusing on local internet marketing with Google, local directories, and local review sites;
- having a presence on social media such as Twitter and social networks such as Facebook – talking about things relevant to the local consumer to engage their interest;
- running in-store or online competitions;
- sponsoring local charities, getting involved in the community, eg doing something with schools, colleges or nursing homes;
- running open events or providing special in-store days;
- making the most of your shop front, especially the window, highlighting featured products and promotions;
- making more of the store interior by focusing on your promotions and point of sale.

The list could go on and you can get very inventive if you want to!

Notice there is a considerable focus on *local* – that's because as a smaller business you should be aiming to serve customers within a reasonable catchment area. If you are in a highly seasonal location, with lots of tourist visitors, they will *still* be interested in finding out more about the facilities in the area local to where they will be visiting. If you are an online-only retailer and have the ability to ship goods nationally then you might be able to operate at a more generic, national level. However, national marketing is much more costly and it would be wise to focus on a couple of highly relevant locations, places 'where your customers are' when it comes to your marketing. This will ensure you attract the right kind of customer, increasing your conversion rate.

My advice would be to test a few of the methods I've listed above to see which best engage more of your ideal customer. You will need to make sure you have a way to measure response rate or the outcome. Without this the results will be of no benefit to you. One of the biggest failures in big companies when it comes to marketing spend is lack of clarity about how to measure return on spend. I've often heard businesses saying they're continuing to spend literally millions on advertising via a certain medium, not because they know what the benefit is, more because of the risk of losing sales should they stop! That's crazy! You must never fall into that trap. If you can't figure out a way to measure response rate to a marketing activity then don't do it (unless it doesn't cost anything).

My second piece of advice is to invest in some PR. Your brand may benefit from PR but I am rather a fan of *you*, the business owner, making more of *your* story, *your* profile. Think about it. Who is the figurehead of the business? Who is the driving force, the passion, the reason it exists? Who is responsible for making it happen, for providing customers with access to products and services, for providing employment? *You are.* As a smaller business you have the unique advantage of a clear 'personality' at the helm. Don't fall into the trap of thinking that if you become the figurehead, the face of the business, then you become a bottleneck potentially reducing the saleability of your business. That's not so – it's subtly different from you *doing* everything. You become someone that people identify with and begin to like. You will attract customers, suppliers and advocates more if you become the face of your brand. Don't believe me? Let's think about this.

Who is the figurehead of Virgin Atlantic? Love him or hate him, Richard Branson is regarded around the world as a hugely successful entrepreneur and leader. Do you think he flies the planes? Of course not; he is, however, synonymous with the Virgin brands and would remain so even if he sold the business.

Test this thinking on a few more mega-brands and you'll see why your profile as the business owner is important. Think through this list of very well-known global brands. If you ask the 'man on the street' to name the owner/founder of the company you'll be surprised at just how many people would know the correct answer!

- Microsoft – Bill Gates
- Google – Larry Page
- Facebook – Mark Zuckerberg
- The Body Shop – Anita Roddick
- Apple – Steve Jobs.

Although Anita Roddick and Steve Jobs are no longer with us, the rest of these people are currently alive and actively involved with their brands. I guarantee you that none of them is, or ever was, considered to be a bottleneck in their business or a barrier to its sale.

So you need to work on your personal profile. Tell the local press about the good things you do in the community. Blog about issues in the community and be an activist for what you believe in. Create 'brand you' and become an expert in your field. Sarah Decent of Modish does this by regularly blogging about the weird and wonderful in the world of shoe design. Her blog illustrates her passion for her product and centres her in her business as the woman behind the brand.

I can sympathize with you if you are unsure about this. I personally used to believe that if I became the face of my businesses I would be seen as a 'small company' – not one that a bigger brand would want to buy from. I was concerned it might deter customers as they may see me as 'risky'. I made the mistake of confusing being seen as the figurehead with being seen as the only resource! It was only after I was introduced to a fantastic lady, Sue Blake, whose background had been traditional PR for over 20 years, that I learned this need not be the case. Sue now focuses on helping business owners to raise their profile – as experts, as people in the public eye. When I stood up as the face of my business, and increased my personal visibility, implementing Sue's advice, I saw a significant increase in interest (attraction) and sales (conversion). Since then I've referred Sue on to a couple of my clients. One in particular, Sadia, the founder of Being U who I mentioned before, found that it was *her* profile, as the person behind a new business, that got the media's attention and not just her innovative products as she might have expected. Sadia has Sue to thank for pushing her to become the face and voice of her brand; I'd ask you to think about doing the same.

Before we move on to consider the 'noise' that other people can create for you I want you to look at how you can plan your 'attraction' campaign. I use a marketing calendar template with my clients – this is based on the promotional calendar, taking that down to the next level of detail, indicating what marketing activities will take place, when, and if these are connected to a promotion or event. Separately I advise they keep track of all costs for an activity and track response rate as a result – thus being able to measure the return on spend of any activity.

Below is the promotional calendar we looked at in Step 5, with the additional content around marketing events. This is the same version that's available in the resources at **www.retailchampion.co.uk/resources** – it's called 'template marketing and promotional calendar'.

You should create a similar planner for your business.

That wraps up on the 'noise' you can make yourself. Let's look at what other people can do.

TABLE 7.1   The example promotional calendar from Step 5, now developed into a combined template marketing and promotional calendar

Month	Calendar events	Academic calendar	Other religious holidays	Sporting events	Promotional activity	Marketing activity
January	New Year	Back to school			End-of-season sale	Window advertising for end of season; new range launch event
February	Valentine's	Half term			Valentine's window feature	Radio advertising about buying the perfect Valentine's gift for a loved one
March	Mother's Day				Mother's Day window feature	Radio advertising about buying the Mother's Day gift

TABLE 7.1 *continued*

Month	Calendar events	Academic calendar	Other religious holidays	Sporting events	Promotional activity	Marketing activity
April	Easter	School holiday – Easter		London Marathon	Price promotion – make your money go further in school holiday theme	Sponsor a local charitable Easter-egg hunt
May	2 × bank holidays	Half term			Re-merchandise to focus on high-summer items	Window and in-store events to focus on the summer ranges
June	Queen's Diamond Jubilee			Wimbledon	Voucher promotion for loyal customer; celebrating the Jubilee	Support local street parties and events; leaflet drop the neighbourhood to promote events
July		School holiday – summer		London Olympics	Two-month event in-store, windows and range of special offers about the Olympics *and* end-of-season sale	Spend some time focusing on online content – updating local directories, Google places listings and tidying up social media pages
August	Late summer bank holiday		Eid			
September		Back to school			Back-to-school window	Flyer to all the local schools to go into school bags offering special discounts on presentation of the flyer
October	Halloween	Half term	Diwali		Halloween and bonfire window	Support local Halloween occasion as sponsor or donate raffle prizes

TABLE 7.1   *continued*

Month	Calendar events	Academic calendar	Other religious holidays	Sporting events	Promotional activity	Marketing activity
November	Bonfire Night				Christmas window	Support local fireworks occasion as sponsor or donate raffle prizes
December	Christmas	School holiday – Christmas	Hanukkah		Gift promotions – tactical, as required!	Big campaign, multiple media, focusing on Christmas gifting, in-store events, late openings, etc

'Noise' other people can make for you

Essentially this is all about word of mouth. We've touched on this in the earlier part of the chapter; these days, with tools like Facebook and Twitter you can really amplify the effect of word of mouth. Used effectively, social media and social networks allow your happy loyal customers, and other advocates of your business, to spread the word about what you offer and why they would recommend that their friends, family, colleagues and contacts visit your shop.

Most of these tools are free to use – although it is advisable if you are not up to speed with these new marketing methods to seek expert advice before diving in, just to avoid wasting time or doing more harm than good. Social media marketing should be an integral part of your brand marketing and internet marketing strategy. Sadly, as with lots of 'new things' a myriad of self-appointed social media experts have come to market, promising that they'll transform the fortunes of your business by showing you how best to use Facebook, Twitter or blogging. I am extremely cautious of these claims. Social media are not a quick fix; they are a tool that enables you to reach more people more quickly. It takes time, effort and the right approach. If you do decide to get some training or advice, make sure you select who you work with very carefully. Go through the process of speaking to their customers to understand if they will meet the promises that they make to you; find out if the results they promise can be measured.

I don't want to put you off – I've personally found that social media have been of tremendous importance to my businesses. I've been using them for business and professional reasons since 2005 when I first created my profile on LinkedIn. Just remember, social media are really only another tool for communicating, sharing and conversing with people. As long as you can speak to a customer in your shop you can use social media to communicate. One of the key success factors is authenticity – being true to yourself, being true to your brand. Some people fall foul of trying to project an 'image' on social media. The trouble is when it comes to the crunch they don't match up to the image that they projected, which can lead to disappointment and distrust.

One word of caution – if you do start using social media for your business you have to be sure you can keep it up. Once a brand develops an engaged audience the last thing it should do is suddenly disappear, go quiet, fail to respond. If you aren't sure you can keep your presence going just yet then hold back until you can.

I am in a rather special position when it comes to all things to do with the internet – I co-own e-mphasis internet marketing, which my husband, Andrew, runs day to day. As we share an office I'm constantly hearing about new trends, developments, opportunities and success stories. I consider myself internet savvy; but then when I look at what his team know compared to my knowledge I am blown away! It's always the case – if you look to someone with considerably more knowledge or experience than you it can be a bit daunting. Don't try to do everything all at once; if you are new to using these tools pick one, learn it, make it work, make sure you feel comfortable with it before adding a second.

When you have your social media in place you can of course then start to encourage customers, suppliers and other advocates of your business to leave positive reviews and recommendations. You can ask them to share your content – your blog, for example – with their connections. Your engaged audience will help you to extend your reach and, over time, the size of your direct audience will increase as a result.

So, using the direct and indirect methods you should now have 'made some noise', drawn attention to your brand, and attracted some potential customers. Are they the *right* kind of customers?

You don't just want footfall, you want the right footfall

Earlier in this chapter I touched on the need to ensure you are attracting the right kind of customer. In the previous chapter I promised I'd share a case study about one of my clients that illustrates why attracting too much of the wrong kind of footfall can just drain your resources.

So this is the story of a client who told me about the experience they had at a major consumer show in London: the Ideal Home Show in 2011. Many months in advance she had booked a stand to exhibit in the 'Ideal Shopping' area, a marketplace for visitors to purchase items as they browsed the show.

On the first weekend the show was immensely busy, but my client told me that exhibitors unanimously reported sales were a fraction of previous years.

The fact is that high footfall doesn't necessarily translate to higher sales. Only an increase in the right kind of footfall (or traffic on an e-commerce site) will increase turnover. In fact, if you throw enough of the wrong kind of visitors at your retail channels all you'll see is a negative impact on your conversion rates. This is exactly what was happening at the Ideal Home Show in 2011. Let me explain why.

The Ideal Home Show produces a monthly magazine. In the month prior to the show a free ticket to attend had been included. That publication was distributed to approximately 250,000 readers. Evidently, readers who may have thought twice about attending, perhaps due to the ticket cost, decided to take advantage of this offer. Many people who otherwise would not have attended (they were not serious buyers) decided that a free ticket meant a cheap and entertaining day out.

So, the exhibitors, who had spent thousands of pounds (in some cases tens of thousands) to have their stand, staffing and materials on display, were inundated with visitors. Sales were not forthcoming and yet visitor numbers were up. Of course these were not the visitors who would usually come to the show specifically to buy. Perhaps the serious buyers were over-looked in the crowds as the stallholders struggled to cope with so many visitors.

This story should illustrate the point about attracting the right kind of consumer. Hopefully the ideas about how to create more attention for *your* business will mean you avoid issues like those experienced by the traders at the Ideal Home Show. While the wrong kind of footfall merely ties up your resources, more of the *right* footfall leads to a higher rate of conversion – so let's move on to that now.

Convert

You've attracted potential customers, now it is your responsibility to convert them. This is your duty! You've got them interested and they want to buy from you; they will be disappointed if they leave you empty-handed. Don't disappoint them. If you have that belief when you are speaking to potential customers, and encourage your staff to believe the same, you will never feel like you're 'giving the hard sell'. If you've attracted them in based on promises on which you can definitely deliver, conversion should be very straightforward.

In fact, converting a customer who has been attracted for all the right reasons is more about being there *to facilitate them in converting themselves* rather than using any specific influencing tactics. Obviously some gentle suggestions, some product recommendations, some cross-selling and up-selling won't go amiss, but this should be used only to enhance their decision to buy and increase the amount they buy.

When it comes to conversion the same theory can be applied online as in-store. Your website should be created so that it can facilitate the sale, providing all the information that a sales assistant would have to hand, making suggestions and recommendations for complementary products and, most importantly, making it very easy to complete the transaction.

Regardless of channel, you've not successfully converted a potential customer into a customer until you have their cash and they have your product. So here is a question to consider:

- Do you measure customer conversion rates through each of your channels?

Just in case you aren't clear about what a conversion rate is, it is simply the number of transactions made in a given period of time divided by the number of people visiting in the same period (footfall or website traffic).

As with the question about attraction, make sure you answer this honestly. If you don't do it, think about how you could. If you already do it, think about what you might need to do to increase the conversion rates. Keep hold of those thoughts – you can include them in your action plan.

In order for attraction to lead to conversion there are a handful of 'ingredients' you need to have in place. These include:

- the right choice of products to meet a customer's needs;
- stock available of the item they want;
- pricing and promotions consistent with what they expect;
- any after-sales services that they might expect – this will depend on what you have explicitly promised in your product information, marketing, point-of-sale materials, etc.

It's not that complex, but of course you'd be amazed how many retailers, large and small, spend a fortune on marketing and then simply don't have the product available when the customer wants to purchase it! Having stock available isn't necessarily the most obvious part of the customer service equation, but it is expected. If you don't have stock of the products that you have led a customer to expect to find in your shop, you cannot convert the sale. Remember the customer service mantra from Step 2, positioning? *When your brand makes promises, implied or explicit, these set expectations with your customer. If you fail to deliver on those promises you will fail to deliver the expected customer experience.*

Being out of stock is a service failure. This and other service failures will impact your customer retention, which we will look at now.

Retain

Now you've won a new customer over. That was quite an effort, all the ingredients that make up your business working together harmoniously to secure a sale and a new customer. In an ideal world you're far better off retaining the customers you've already won over than having to start from the attraction stage time and time again. You'll never grow your business if you don't retain customers and all your energy will be in constantly attracting new customers. The key to successful retailing is to both retain your existing customers *and* attract new customers. A good friend of mine, Grant Leboff, talks about an upside-down funnel in his book *Sticky Marketing*.

FIGURE 7.2   Customer retention and the 'reverse funnel' thinking, developed by Grant Leboff, author of *Sticky Marketing*

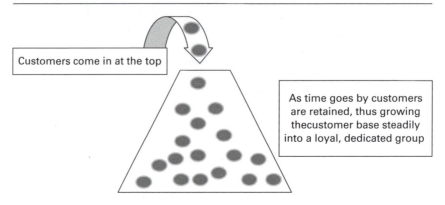

Customers come in at the top

As time goes by customers are retained, thus growing thecustomer base steadily into a loyal, dedicated group

It's a great way to think about how you should grow your business and your customer base over time.

How do you retain customers?

The best place to start is by asking your existing, loyal customers what it is that keeps them coming back. If you can get them to spend some time talking to you then you can try to identify if it is product, pricing, service, location, something else or a bit of all of those reasons that makes them want to buy from you. Don't make the conversation feel like an interrogation, though! Keep it light, genuine and flowing; respect their time – they may have other more pressing priorities than to provide you with insights into what makes them tick. You'll have to use your judgement so as to avoid alienating the very people who are most important to your business. Get it right, however, and the benefit is twofold. Everything you learn in speaking to your regular, loyal customers, especially those who are your 'ideal customer', can be reused in your marketing to attract more of the same (already commencing part of the upward spiral). In addition it will point you in the right direction to increase retention. You should try to identify three types of feedback from this insight:

1 what your business needs to keep doing, and potentially do more of;
2 what it needs to stop doing;
3 what it needs to begin doing.

If you solicit this kind of feedback from your customers regularly then you'll be able to continually adapt to your customers' changing needs and desires.

If you have not yet started trading then the next best thing to going through the exercise above is to speak to your friends, family, connections – in fact anyone who you consider to be similar to your ideal customer. You should be asking them to explain things like: What are the attributes of the brands that they are loyal to? Why do they remain loyal? What is it that's different between these brands and the brands they don't like or are not loyal to? If you can piece together an 'identikit' view of the attributes that would create loyalty for your ideal customer you can make sure you include these in your future business operating model.

Loyalty programmes

Some retailers believe that the only way to retain customers is to implement a loyalty programme. My take on this is that when you go through the thinking processes outlined above you'll know if a loyalty programme will or will not be relevant, or desirable, to your ideal customers. Not all retailers need loyalty programmes; for some it's great, for others an unnecessary admin overhead.

If you do decide to develop a loyalty programme I would suggest you think about who it is for, and why. Before you dive in it's important to really know the customer, to understand and measure their cross-channel shopping behaviour with you, in order to get the loyalty proposition exactly right for them.

This process actually starts at the point of new customer acquisition – you need to have some method of capturing the customer details, and the source of the customer (eg radio advert, flyer, online marketing, etc). You need to do this because if you want to measure their cross-channel behaviour you have to 'know' them from the first time they transact with you. In addition, in order to understand the value of your marketing you need to know the source of new customers and the amount they have spent with you since you attracted them.

With a reasonable CRM tool even a small retailer can discover information about their customers; such as if their cross-channel customers are likely to spend more with them than a single-channel customer. Additionally, CRM can help you to define the offers you could be making to past customers based on the items that best complement their past purchases. This is where it can be highly beneficial in terms of increasing customer loyalty. By understanding and analysing a customer's transactions through all channels the retailer can provide promotions, information and special offers that demonstrate they know and understand their customer. In turn, thanks to the convenience of receiving relevant, appropriate marketing messages from the retailer the customer will spend again. CRM and loyalty tools do take some time to set up but this is another element that a small business, with plans to grow, should be putting in place.

Now for another question:

- Do you have a process to increase customer retention and reward loyalty?

You might not feel that you need to reward loyalty but you should be looking at methods to increase retention:

- Do you understand how often your existing customers come back to you?
- Do you have a view as to what they spend with you each year?
- If you could bring them back more often would that increase your sales?

If you spend some time analysing this, assuming you have the data, then you may get some ideas as to what steps to take to increase the frequency of visit and therefore their spend with you. If you don't yet have the data then begin to think about what you would like to know, how that information would help you, and therefore what data you need to keep and what analysis you need to perform to get to that level of understanding. Wherever you are at in this process, add something to your action plan that will enable you to move forward and improve this area.

Role of social media in customer retention

Social media had a role to play in attraction, as discussed above. They are also relevant in retention. If your customers' preferred method of communication is via social networks then should they attempt to communicate with you, for example on Facebook, you need to be quick to respond. If a customer thanks you or recommends you then you need to acknowledge them and thank them for their endorsement. If a customer complains on social media it is absolutely imperative that you address it quickly, openly, honestly and with good grace. You'll be surprised: in the attraction process brands who may have had bad feedback but who addressed it well are forgiven. Those who ignored the problem or tried to make excuses are not trusted. Finally, if you annoy or upset a customer, but then manage to resolve the situation to their satisfaction, they are likely to not only stay loyal but also to tell people about how you fixed a problem! Monitoring social media for consumer comment about your brand is critical. Remember to thank those who endorse you and to try to turn a negative feedback into a positive experience.

Role of service delivery in retention

In the section above I mentioned the importance of dealing with complaints and how that can actually enhance retention. Before we move off this topic and onto recommendations I want to look at the factors that contribute to the service experience and how that impacts your ability to retain customers. In Step 5, pricing and promotions, I commented: 'If you can't compete on price, compete on service.' The truth is that a smaller retailer has the opportunity to deliver a much more personalized customer-service experience than a major chain; so you should leverage that advantage.

There are, however, a few issues with this. I've listed a couple, and offered some resolutions in the table below. If you can think of more, add them to the list and try to think of a possible resolution.

TABLE 7.2   Issues and possible resolutions for a retailer leveraging service delivery in the customer-retention process

Issue	Possible resolution
As the retailer you have no idea about the unique expectation in the mind of each customer. What disappoints one will delight another.	You can best mitigate this risk by really making your positioning and all of your customer communications clear. Even so, sometimes it won't work out as you planned. Just remember, you can't please all of the people all of the time. Focus on the ones you *did* delight, while learning and understanding why you disappointed another.
Each branch manager, team member, part-timer, delivery driver – in fact anyone representing your business at the point of service – has the ability to impact, positively or negatively, on that customer's experience. These 'moments of truth' are important in leaving the right lasting impression.	Training the team. Share the vision, values, mission and positioning. Ensure they understand what that means to them in their job. It's worth the investment of time to ensure they understand how you want your customers treated and how they contribute to the retention process.

Fundamentally it all boils down to the fact that customers like to be cared about. In a heavily contested market where the consumer is cautious about who they spend their money with, the kind of service they get from their 'friendly, local, independent... whoever' really matters. It can really set you apart from the bigger retailers. It isn't necessarily about the highest standards; you just need to make sure your customers understand what they get from you, and what they don't. Only then can they judge if their experiences match your promises.

When it comes to service, as I mentioned above, do it right, consistently, and they'll love you so much that they'll start to recommend you to their friends, family and social network. So let's look in more detail at recommendations; that's the final step in the four-part cycle of customer engagement.

Recommend

Achieving a level of customer engagement such that your customers are willing to recommend and refer you is proof that you have repeatedly delivered your promises. Don't rest on your laurels, though – if you then have a failure they will not only be disappointed but potentially also embarrassed to have suggested you to their network. If you want to engage your customers, to attract, convert and retain them, you will have a responsibility to them, and to keeping the promises you made.

When customers start to recommend your business you have essentially created a whole team of unpaid salespeople out in the field. They are your most valuable assets and you should reward them with thanks and, if appropriate, something of value.

Some retailers I know have successfully implemented a 'recommend-a-friend' scheme. For example, if a regular customer brings a friend then they both get 10 per cent off their purchases. Some retailers have incorporated this as part of an event or special occasion that thanks loyal customers by providing a fun, social occasion in-store with special offers and promotions *and* the opportunity to bring a friend.

There are different ways to reward customers for their recommendations. For some it may not be necessary; customers may be perfectly happy to spread the word about you just because they're grateful to you for providing them with excellent service.

Don't miss the opportunity to harness their positivity – you should ask them to provide a testimonial on one of the online review sites (over 75 per cent of consumers are influenced by reviews from past customers). You can also use their feedback in your own marketing and PR, to give other potential customers confidence to buy from you.

A final question:

- Do you encourage happy customers to recommend your business to others?

Be honest again – if you don't then it is a simple quick win, you can start immediately! You might want to set up a profile on a customer review website; perhaps an industry-specific one, eg for the travel industry, tripadvisor is the leading review site. Having a profile on a review website, and being able to direct happy customers to a 'place' to leave a review, will make it easier for them to do it for you. When they do leave a review it creates a repository of recommendations all about your brand.

If you already ask for recommendations, are you successful? Do you have a 'place' where you can invite them to leave their feedback? If you aren't getting as many reviews/recommendations as you'd like, look at the method that you use to capture their comments – perhaps it needs improvement. Think this over, and identify what actions you need to take to increase positive feedback about your business.

Recommendations are pretty straightforward; it's getting to that level of engagement that takes the effort. Once achieved, you'll have completed the first cycle of your upward spiral of customer engagement. Those customer recommendations now add to the other aspects of your customer attraction process. And so you continue upwards: attract, convert, retain, recommend – your business will be booming!

Summing up

At the start I said that I believed this step is the one where as a smaller retailer you can really make your mark. We started out by considering the concept of 'being where your customers are' from the perspective of brand visibility and findability. You should now have a good idea as to what media are most appropriate for you to reach your potential customers. In this section I also pointed out that even if you don't yet have a transactional website you should not underestimate the importance of the internet.

Then, and for the body of the chapter, we've looked at my four-part customer engagement cycle, with most emphasis on the first and third steps: attraction and retention. Along the way I asked you to reflect on the following questions:

- Do you know what attracted your existing customers?
- Do you measure customer conversion rates through each of your channels?
- Do you have a process to increase customer retention and reward loyalty?
- Do you encourage happy customers to recommend your business to others?

I hope you found these thought provoking and that the outcome has enabled you to think of several things you should be doing, which will now become part of your action plan.

The success of your business will depend on how you engage your customer. I promised that it would be as important to your business as knowing what products to sell, for what price and through which channels. By completing this step you have got all the ingredients to successfully sell to customers.

The final three steps, 8 – supply chain, 9 – planning and controlling, and 10 – back office, are about 'oiling the wheels', so to speak. These steps help you to make sure the business 'flows' and that all the necessary infrastructure is in place to *allow* you to sell more product to more customers.

Step 8 is not going to focus on how, or what, to sell, but what to buy, from where, and how to get it to where you need it. Let's get going!

Step Eight
Supply chain

Introduction

Step 8 is all about managing the supply chain: an important ingredient in delivering on your service promise. In Step 4 you identified the ideal range, in Step 5 you determined the ideal price, in 6 you decided which channels you'd sell through and what delivery proposition you would offer, in 7 you engaged the customer. **In Step 8 you, your suppliers, and any third parties involved in the process, have to deliver on all of those promises!**

Until now we've done a lot of planning and spent all the time focusing on the proposition, positioning and customer experience. Now it's crunch time – the quality of your sourcing and supply-chain process will mean you either can live up to the promises you've made to your customer, or you can't.

I started my retail head office career with M&S and much of my role was focused on management of the inbound flow of stock. People only ever noticed us when something went wrong. This is the thankless nature of supply-chain management – rather like our expectation to have a phone signal, running water, electricity: they're only really noticeable in their absence. In retail, the supply chain is *very* noticeable when it fails!

During my early career I had countless 'debates' with marketing about which function was more important. I would say, 'Ah, but without us in supply chain you'd have no product to sell, it wouldn't be on time, on quality, at the right price,' and they would say, 'Ah, but without us in marketing you'd have no reason to buy, you'd have no customers, no demand and no business.'

Of course, we were both right.

However, most of the retail business owners that I have met, and that's a lot of people, have little passion for the supply-chain or sourcing processes. They're people and product focused; are you? I think one of the primary drivers to start up a retail business for most of the business owners I've met is because they love the product and they love the interactions with their team and the general public. Not one has ever suggested that they love supplier negotiations or the planning, tracking and managing of stock flow around their business.

Luckily I do love that – because I know how important this part of the process is. That's probably got a great deal to do with growing up in a family of retailers! My parents sourced their raw materials and 'owned' the whole supply chain from creation of the product to delivery to the customer. The smooth running of the end-to-end supply chain *was* fundamental to profitability. In my parents' business if there was no availability of a popular fabric, sales would drop. If a machine failed in the factory, orders would be delayed and customers would complain or demand refunds. The office team who should have been receiving and processing orders were bogged down letting customers know that there would be a delay. When the supply-chain 'system' failed, the repercussions were wide reaching and impacted on profitability. So the reason I love supply chain is because when you get it right it makes everything else so much easier and so much more efficient.

In this chapter I've broken the sourcing and supply-chain processes into three areas. There are entire books written on supply-chain management – when I was completing my professional diploma for the Chartered Institute of Purchasing and Supply (MCIPS) I had to read at least 10 of them! These are very detailed, very dry, and focus at a level that would only really be relevant for global mega-brands: oil giants and international pharmaceuticals businesses, for instance. In the most part these texts are not even relevant to large retailers, let alone smaller businesses. Thus the three areas I've picked to explore are a taster of the three key things that *will* make a difference to a smaller retailer.

These include:

● selecting a supplier;

● managing the relationship;

● managing physical logistics.

In the first section, selecting a supplier, we'll consider who and where you buy your merchandise from. You might want to ask yourself a few questions, such as: Are they ethical? Can you get the quality you want and the volumes you need? We'll delve into all the questions you need to ask of your supplier to make sure you are sourcing your goods from a reputable place.

In this section we'll also look at how your supplier strategy meets your goals, mission, values and beliefs, eg if you feel you should be sourcing locally or are happy to buy globally, etc.

When we take a look at the supplier relationship we'll be looking at what you can do to ensure that you make their life as easy as possible, communicating your requirements so that they can in turn meet your requests. We'll look at how you can keep track of your critical path and your supplier performance. Also in this section we'll consider some possibilities when it comes to negotiations – buying terms, quantities, etc.

Finally we'll look at how to manage the physical logistics, the flow of goods from your supplier to the end destination, whether that be your store or direct to your customer. We'll look at this in four stages:

1 inbound transport;

2 storage;

3 outbound distribution;

4 reverse logistics.

At the end of this chapter you should feel more confident about the elements that you need to have in place to better understand, manage and control your supply chain in order that it can perform its role in meeting your service delivery promises.

So, let's now take a good look at selecting a supplier.

Selecting a supplier

One of the most important considerations you'll have to make when buying anything, not only your products for resale, is who to choose to be your supplier.

When it comes to product you may well have a choice of sales agents, wholesalers and the manufacturer direct when it comes to sources of supply. With product purchases you need to know:

● Can they provide the product(s) you want?

● Does the order-to-delivery lead time fit your needs?

● Can they supply the quantity you want, both the initial order and any subsequent replenishment orders?

● Can this all be achieved for a price that makes it viable for you – is there sufficient scope for mark-up such that the retail price fits in with your price architecture?

From the range plan you should know what products you want. You know when you plan to launch your new items; therefore you can work backwards from launch date to plan when you should order them based on the delivery lead time. In Step 9 we'll look at the forward planning, so that you can determine if you should be buying the full season stock upfront, or if you can bring in an initial quantity and top up with replenishment orders (this will also depend on supplier minimums – we'll look at that later in this chapter). You'll know what price points are acceptable based on your margin targets and price architecture. So, with all this information to hand you can very quickly determine if a supplier should be ruled into, or ruled out of, further consideration.

For any purchases, from professional services (lawyer, accountant, HR advisor, designer, PR, internet marketing, etc) to support services (call centre, parcel carrier, IT support, etc) and from consumables (carrier bags, till roll, toilet paper, etc) to capital expenses (interior fit out, IT hardware and software, etc) to product for resale (your merchandise) you should be considering your options, getting quotes and meeting suppliers to understand if they are a good 'fit' for your business as well as able to provide your requirements.

Many of the principles you would apply to selecting suppliers for your merchandise requirements would also apply to selecting a supplier for all manner of other things.

In the same way that we talked about how you would engage your customers, the importance of reviews and references, consider what your supplier needs to do to engage *you* as a customer. Create a checklist of your expectations from your supplier. I don't just mean the ability to provide the volume of products or services that you want to an acceptable quality standard, on time and at a fair price, either – that's the bare minimum to make it onto the shortlist for consideration in the first place. What I mean is all of the various other things that matter to you, for example:

- Are they considered ethical? Are their green credentials important to you?
- Are they familiar with businesses like yours? Do they have sector expertise?
- Do they come highly recommended by people you would trust?
- Do they offer any guarantees? Are they adequately insured?
- What after-sales service do they offer? What is the service-level agreement?
- If something went wrong do they have any relevant support lines/help centre? What is the availability of access to that service?
- Are there any 'hidden costs' such as premium-rate numbers for accessing support and/or hourly charges for resolving service failures?
- Is there any risk of *your* business being attacked for working with the supplier? Have you investigated them sufficiently to ensure they are compliant with all reasonable standards?
  - Think about the *huge* issues faced by major retail brands over the years when allegations were made against them in the media about working with suppliers whose factories employed child labour. Even when the claims were proven to have been inaccurate there was irreparable damage done to the retailers in question. You can't afford for anything like that to impact your business!

I am sure you can add to this list with factors that really matter to you.

Another aspect of supplier selection is to consider how your choice of supplier meets your goal, mission, values and beliefs. Even if you have a supplier that 'ticks all the boxes' above, if you simply don't feel that they are 'right for you' then the relationship will be strained at best; likely as not it won't work.

Think through the other aspects that matter to you; perhaps if you can't find all of the ingredients you'd compromise, perhaps not. It's your business; you have to be comfortable with who you choose to spend your money with in exactly the same way that your customers need to feel comfortable spending their money with you.

In my experience it makes sense to have a rigorous process to go through when choosing a supplier. You need to literally be able to 'tick all the boxes'. As mentioned, the minimum requirement is the ability to supply to your requirements, on time and for an acceptable price. Beyond that there is a great deal you need to be considering to avoid risks of supply-chain failure, and thus potentially a failure to meet your customers' expectations.

Take some time to write *your* list of questions for a potential supplier. Make sure this is on your action plan. You don't have to ask these questions of the supplier directly; but you should do sufficient research into them so that you feel certain your questions have been answered. Make sure you include everything that matters – from the attributes that align a supplier more closely to your goals, values and beliefs to the attributes that remove your risk of doing business with them.

Finally, and to avoid any ambiguity or confusion, it is wise to have, as a minimum, a simple letter of agreement. This could be a statement of commitment from both sides. This will protect you from exposure to some risks and prove to your supplier that you are a serious businessperson. If you are ever asked to enter into a longer-term service agreement with a supplier, and a more 'weighty' contract is handed to you, seek expert advice. A good commercial lawyer will have professional indemnity insurance that protects *you* if their advice is flawed (you can sue their insurance for your losses if you can demonstrate their advice was flawed). In addition, what you spend on their fee (and be prepared, a good lawyer will charge a high hourly rate) should be easily recovered through having had a contract reviewed, negotiated and revised with your best interests in mind. Certainly *never* sign anything you don't understand – nine times out of ten it won't matter, but on the one occasion it matters you can be certain it will *really* matter! Such is the nature of these things! I like taking a few risks in business, but signing contracts that commit me to spending with a supplier over a period of time is one area I'd never take a risk on!

Negotiations *could* be part of the selection process; however, if a supplier is the right supplier for you and you've done all the necessary analysis of their basic pricing compared to your requirements, I don't believe it is necessary at the selection stage to enter into a negotiation. Negotiations are not one-sided; they are about finding a mutually acceptable position on a point for debate. This is why I've chosen to cover supplier negotiations in the next aspect of your supply-chain processes: managing the supplier relationship.

Managing the relationship

In this section we're going to look specifically at your product suppliers. While the selection process we just walked through *could* be used on non-product suppliers the focus in this section is really about making sure you get product for resale available to your customers through your channels. We'll look more closely at three interrelated areas. We'll firstly look at why good communications and information sharing between you and your supplier will enable them to serve you better. Then we'll look at managing the critical path, which is of particular importance if you have the past-season stock on clearance and are planning a big launch of the new-season range. Then we'll look at the negotiations, considering various elements of the relationship, where you might ask for support from a supplier and what they might need in return from you to make that workable for them.

So, firstly, let's look at communication, collaboration and information sharing.

Retail supplier collaboration

In the bigger retailers it is now generally accepted that there has been a shift away from what were in the past quite adversarial relationships with suppliers. Best practice is all about building successful, long-term relationships across the retail supply chain through the sharing of key information between all of the actors in the supply chain – often referred to as supplier collaboration. Essentially this approach adds value when retailer and supplier are working together towards a common goal – it doesn't work if there is a power struggle and one or other party uses a balance of power in negotiations.

Now I don't believe that this relationship style is *only* suited to the bigger players – far from it – I think smaller businesses can benefit enormously from working in a similar way with their supplier base. The boot may be on the other foot, your suppliers may be much bigger than you, but that doesn't change the fact that by building professional relationships you can work together more effectively.

When you work closely with your suppliers, communicate openly with them and share information about your business performance and plans, they can really help you. They have a great deal of market knowledge and can give their perspective to you, which can help inform your decision-making processes. For instance, when it comes to range planning you can get quite a lot of insight from your suppliers. You can speak to those you know well and ask them about the products they have that may interest you. Explain your thoughts about your range direction and your ideal customer – who you are buying for. You'll be surprised: your suppliers may be more than happy to share insights with you about the marketplace – and they will have more of a 'total market view' because as a supplier they deal with many retailers; not just you.

Why collaborate? What is the benefit to the end-to-end supply chain?

Sharing sales data is also becoming more commonplace between suppliers and retailers. The real benefits come about when the retailer is providing the supplier with information relating to their products' performance in terms of sales/stock/future demand/promotional effectiveness, etc. For the supplier some information, even if a little inaccurate, is better than none at all when it comes to their own supply-chain planning. When the retailer shares plans with their supplier, the supplier is better able to supply. As a result the supplier is more likely to give the retailer consistency and security of supply. All parties are well informed and the supply chain is able to flow efficiently. It is usually only the knee-jerk reactions or uncommunicated events that cause a costly impact throughout the supply-chain system.

Although becoming more commonplace, for many retailers supplier collaboration is still something of a new concept. Many are cautious about sharing sensitive sales data, and rightly so: with fierce competition a bit of healthy paranoia about confidential data getting into the public domain makes a lot of sense! However, more and more retailers are realizing the benefits of working in closer partnership with their suppliers. These benefits are directly visible on the bottom line. Let me tell you how.

When I was completing my MCIPS one of the professors of supply chain said, 'Stock replaces information in the supply chain' – this is so true – because when retailer and supplier don't communicate effectively each party holds a bit of safety stock, just in case the other party fails. The retailer holds stock in case the supplier fails to supply in full, the supplier holds stock in case the retailer fails to order in reasonable time, etc. Stock ties up cash, takes up space, and deteriorates in quality over time. If, by being more open and sharing more information, and by working more in partnership, each party could reduce their stockholding that would be of direct commercial benefit to both. Worth considering.

Next we'll take a look at managing the critical path (the dates on which activities *must* happen by in order to keep to a deadline, such as a range launch). The critical path is key to running a successful supply chain, and to the supplier communication process.

Supply-chain critical path tracking

As a retailer you will understand that knowing when products are due to arrive for a new season launch is critical to timing the clearance activities for your old ranges.

That's just the beginning of good supply-chain tracking, though. Ideally you should be keeping a record of when each and every product or order is due to arrive with you, and phoning your suppliers a week or two prior to the due date to confirm everything is still on target. The reason for keeping a close eye on the progress of orders is to help reduce your risk should something not be going to plan.

I am not suggesting that you can necessarily resolve a problem by knowing about it, but you can put in place an effective alternative. For example, if you knew a supplier was going to be late with a shipment of five items you could phone around other suppliers and see if you could get some extra stock of similar items. You could then merchandise the store with a bit more stock of the alternatives, covering up any 'gaps' that the late arrival of the order could have caused.

Also, by having a clear commitment to due dates you are in a much stronger position to cancel a proportion of the order. If a supplier was late delivering items necessary for a key promotion or event, and now the opportunity to sell those items has passed, you would be quite within your rights to discuss cancelling the order because they had failed to meet their commitment and now you no longer have the ability to sell the stock.

Keeping track of dates and progress is like having an early-warning mechanism in place, allowing you to mitigate the risk of supply-chain problems. I am sure you can see how having the right to cancel chunks of late-arriving stock could be greatly beneficial to both your cash flow and your margin. If you accept stock that really isn't going to sell as planned you're opening yourself up to taking a margin hit should you subsequently need to discount that stock to clear it.

The other benefit of tracking is the ability to maintain a 'supplier scorecard' – a tool to keep an eye on which of your suppliers are regularly failing you, or which are always doing a top job. You can keep a record, by supplier, of the number of times they have either failed to meet due dates or delivered incorrect products/quantities. You can use this in a discussion with a supplier about improving performance; you might even suggest that if they don't improve performance you'll have to take your business elsewhere.

Yes, you might be a small business, but if you treat them professionally and can demonstrate with facts and examples how they need to improve, you will earn their respect *and* see a turnaround in their service levels.

Of course, information about performance can also help you when it comes to negotiations – and that's what we'll look at now.

Supplier negotiations

As I mentioned earlier, you could decide to include negotiations as part of your selection process; and you should certainly negotiate some of the terms if you are committing to long-term contracts. That said, you've still mentally chosen the supplier before you enter into the negotiation – the negotiation is then just about ensuring both parties get the best possible outcome. If you have done all of the necessary preliminary research into the supplier you *will* find a way to work together through a negotiation; it should not reach stalemate, you should not need to go back to the selection process and start again. That's why I include it here as opposed to within the selection process itself.

When it comes to product suppliers especially, there really is little sense in even beginning to consider a negotiation as part of the selection process. It's not until you're talking about initial order quantities, due dates, delivery charges, terms of business, replenishment quantities and the like, that you're going to be in much of a position to know what terms you'd like to discuss in more detail. If you have found a supplier you are keen to work with, who has products you'd like to stock, then the negotiation is an ongoing discussion every time you want to buy into a new range, and it is to be expected.

Usually negotiations are based on some of the terms of business that if changed would provide you with a more favourable outcome. Almost always when a supplier concedes a point in a negotiation they will ask for something that they believe to be of equal value (to them) in return. You may be lucky – you may get a proposal from a supplier that's exactly what you wanted – payment terms, pricing, minimum order quantities – all 100 per cent in line with your plan. Some people would say that you should still try to negotiate, to try to get a bit more value. It is up to you. I would suggest if your business can achieve its goals without any further negotiation then you should accept the offer. What goes around comes around. On another occasion you may need a favour, and if you've always been challenging you're less likely to get a favour! Plus if you always ask for a bit more here and there, eventually suppliers will begin to add some 'padding' to their pricing or terms of business to accommodate your apparent desire to always 'do a deal'. If you told the supplier, 'On this occasion your proposal is 100 per cent in line with what I was looking for; we don't need to waste time with negotiations,' you've not sounded like a pushover, you've sounded like a serious businessperson who had a clear expectation and who has no interest in 'screwing the supplier down on price' (as many retailers have been accused of in the past!).

What are the areas you might want to negotiate on?

In the table below I've summarized a few ideas around areas you might want to consider negotiating on and the reasons why.

As you can tell from Table 8.1, there are several areas where you might need to negotiate, and with very valid business reasons. There are many more; these are just a few of the more common ones. If you think of others then jot them down and add the reason why that could be of value to you.

If you want a *good* relationship with a supplier, for the long term, don't overdo it – unless something is really important to you, literally a deal breaker, don't push too hard. Remember, there are usually 'several ways to skin a cat' and if you talk to a supplier about the reasons why something is important to you and why the terms proposed can't work, they may come up with a third option that just happens to work a treat for both of you.

TABLE 8.1   Some points where a retailer may engage in negotiations with a supplier and the benefits of a positive outcome

Negotiation point	Benefit to retailer
Cost price	Obviously the easiest way to increase your margins is to reduce your cost price; so long as you are still able to retail the item for the planned recommended retail price.
Delivery charges	If you can mitigate the costs of delivery this is directly beneficial to margin.
Minimum order quantity	Minimums are often something the supplier tries to impose, and understandably: they don't want to be issuing small orders with a low value as the management overhead would mean any margin they are making is quickly eaten up by all the associated admin. As the retailer, however, you too need to consider what is an ideal order quantity. Although receiving stock on a little-and-often basis is good for cash flow it isn't necessarily beneficial for you. Look at the effort you have to make to track the order, make sure it is received, check the quantities, book the invoice on the system, match it to the order on the system and make a payment. Suddenly having slightly less frequent orders, and less admin, can be quite attractive – so only push on minimum order quantities if you feel that they would force you to buy so much stock as to either tie up far too much cash or risk having to carry it forward as a residual line, potentially losing margin due to clearance.

In this chapter I can't teach you much more about negotiation skills; if that's something that worries you I'd suggest you get some training or a specific text to help you with that aspect of your business. Hopefully, you now have a good background about why and when to negotiate and can use this as part of a positive, win–win, approach to your supplier relationships.

That concludes the second section of supply-chain management; the third is a lot more to do with the practical actions within and throughout the supply chain – termed physical logistics.

TABLE 8.1   *continued*

Negotiation point	Benefit to retailer
Payment terms (eg 30 days from receipt)	Payment terms can make a huge difference to your cash flow. If you don't have to pay for the stock until you've already started to sell it then chances are you'll have banked most of the value of the order by the time the invoice is due to be paid. *But* don't forget, your supplier has issued the goods; therefore they are bearing the cost of financing the period between when they had to pay for their raw materials and when you pay for their finished product. This will be accounted for somewhere in the supply chain, so if you can afford to pay on order *and* agree a cost-price reduction in respect of your swift payment, this option might be favourable – it really depends on the cash dynamic in your business and if cash flow or profitability is more important to you at that point in time.
Buying terms (eg sale or return)	There are some suppliers who would be willing to look at more creative terms – sale or return is one way that a smaller supplier can encourage a retailer to show off their product without the risk of carrying residual stock or losing margin in clearance. There are few suppliers who offer this, but if they do then as long as the product is congruent with your range, will make good margin, and you have space for it in your store, there is no reason not to give it a go!
Support services	Some suppliers selling more complex products do have a helpline for retailers/stockists. Some charge for this, others don't. It could be something you might want to include in a negotiation.
Extended warranties	Suppliers may underwrite extended warranties so you can offer your customer three- or five-year warranties either free of charge or for a nominal top-up charge. With complex or high-priced items something like this could be very desirable to your customer and worth working on achieving with your supplier at the negotiation stage.

Managing physical logistics

As I said in the Introduction, in this final part of the chapter we're going to look at how to manage the physical logistics; the flow of goods from your supplier to the end destination, whether that be your store or direct to your customer. We'll look at this in four stages:

1 inbound transport;

2 storage;

3 outbound distribution;

4 reverse logistics.

The reason I'm breaking it down into four stages is because there are potentially different third parties involved in each step, and because there are certainly different considerations, not just from the perspective of the movement of goods but also the associated recording and financial tracking.

Inbound transport

The terms agreed with your supplier will determine if it is them or you who is responsible for booking the delivery of your order to your location. Chances are, however, that neither of you owns the transport; thus you need to bear in mind that the driver needs to have a clear understanding of what they are delivering, to where, for when.

Transport companies are quite unforgiving – if you are not available to receive the order when they are booked to deliver it they are likely to refuse to redeliver without a charge.

Make sure you have a simple booking system – a spreadsheet will do. It should include which orders you expect to be delivered, at what time, on what day, and by which carriers.

If you have stock delivered directly to your store you also need to make sure that you communicate any delivery restrictions. In some high-street locations you may not be allowed to receive a delivery during busy periods; you will need to make sure you explain this to the carrier (if you are booking the inbound delivery) or to the supplier if they are taking care of the arrangements.

Storage

Storage of stock is a necessary requirement of any retail business (other than those in a purely make-to-order model). If you can store everything you need in your store that's fine for the short term, but as you grow you might need to consider a dedicated storage location.

The benefits can be great – you only need to hold minimal stock in each store from which to service sales. You can replenish from your storage location as required. In addition many third-party storage locations will also do pick, pack and despatch for e-commerce orders as well as for your store replenishment.

One word of caution, though. Your stockholding increases if you hold sales cover in multiple locations; you should do a rough calculation of the cost of this additional stock (assuming you can accommodate it in stores anyway) vs cost of storage and transport. When interest rates are low and transport costs are high you might be better off to hold more stock in the stores and cut out a centralized storage facility. As the business expands keep an eye on this; keep checking that the operations you've got in place are still most efficient and most cost effective for your business.

The only drawback to not having a centralized storage location is the aspect of customer order fulfilment, but we'll come on to that next.

Outbound distribution

As touched on above, many third-party logistics providers who can provide storage facilities also provide pick, pack and despatch options, not just to your retail stores but also to customers. This is a great benefit if you can justify the costs. If you find that the cost of storage at present isn't justifiable you can always pick, pack and despatch orders from a store – it's more manual, but if you have the resources to dedicate to processing e-commerce orders once or twice per day, along with easy access to couriers/parcel post, then there is no reason why not.

Of course you intend to grow, that's why we're working through 10 steps to retail success, and therefore there will come a time when you need to ensure that you have adequate infrastructure for your outbound distribution to fulfil store and customer requirements.

Reverse logistics

The last piece of the puzzle is the ability to return goods back through the supply chain. You need to consider how you would process a customer return from an e-commerce customer – how could they send their item back? Where would it be shipped to and how would the item be received, checked and put back into stock? Again, a good third-party logistics provider can also do this for you.

There are also times, certainly when you've got a few stores, that you may need to return stock from stores to your central storage location. You could choose to send seasonal items that you might not want to sell in clearance in-store (think Christmas decorations) back to your storage location. You could then either keep the items in storage and redistribute next year, sell them on eBay (or other clearance channels), or dispose of them if the cost price didn't warrant the management overhead of trying to sell them or keep them. There may be a need to do a product recall – a known fault, for instance. There are a number of reasons why you need a supply chain that can flow in reverse; so bear that in mind when defining your requirements and considering third-party suppliers for these services.

There are whole shelves full of books dedicated to the topic of physical logistics. The key for me was to give you some food for thought – we can't cover the whole range of possibilities for your supply chain in this single chapter.

Summing up

In wrapping up on the topic of supply chain as a whole I'd like you to take some time to reflect on what you'll now do differently as a result of the things that have been covered.

You have now completed Step 8 – supply chain. In this chapter we have broken down the supply chain into three key areas that I believe are most relevant and applicable to smaller businesses. We have worked through:

- selecting a supplier;
- managing the relationship;
- managing physical logistics.

In the first section you'll have spent some time considering what *you* want from your suppliers – what matters to you. You'll have developed a list of questions that you would want to have answered in order to feel comfortable in appointing a supplier.

Next we looked at supplier relationships. We considered how to best share information with suppliers and the benefits that building a more collaborative relationship can have. We also talked about the supply-chain critical path tracking, and how keeping records of supplier performance can be beneficial in knowing who to place your business with in future. We concluded the section on relationships with a few thoughts on negotiations – including a table of negotiation points and what the possible benefit could be to the retailer from negotiating on those points.

Finally, we discussed physical logistics, the flow of goods from your supplier to the end destination, whether that be to your store or direct to your customer. Breaking physical logistics into four stages:

1 inbound transport;
2 storage;
3 outbound distribution;
4 reverse logistics.

We have considered the relevance to your business now and in the future of having a more robust physical logistics flow.

You should now be feeling much more confident about the management of your supply chain and as a result you can ensure that the supply chain doesn't have to take the blame should there be a service failure in future!

We're now ready to move onto Step 9 – planning and controlling.

Step Nine
Planning and controlling

Introduction

Step 9 is all about planning the business, and then monitoring it, in order to stay in control. In many ways this is probably the most important part of the business as this links strategy to operations and provides you with all the information you need in order to make confident, commercially sound decisions.

In this chapter we're going to first consider the importance of planning, the reason why it's worth investing your time in doing the detail. Then we'll take a look at the key planning elements that you should have in place. These will include:

- A high-level business plan: used to set direction and budgets – this is your 'destination' and it will include:
  - top-line sales forecasts;
  - operational costs;
  - some narrative.
- A detailed operating plan: used to manage the business on a daily basis, to keep an eye on cash, costs and sales performance. This is your 'route' to your destination. This will include:
  - using the range plan to develop 'WSSI' (weekly sales, stock and intake plan);
  - using WSSI for stock planning, building in promotional plan;
  - importance of a cash-flow plan;
  - ratio planning (relevant for fashion retailing, or any product area with a size mix to consider).

Whole books have been written about 'how to write a business plan' so that's not the focus of this chapter; what this chapter is about is helping you to identify some key things you should include and that you will need to monitor, and giving you a starting place if this is something a bit new to you.

In the final section we'll consider how to use the plan for analytics, insight, measurement, controlling and reporting. We'll touch on tools, but that's something we'll consider in more depth when we look at IT in Step 10. We'll wrap up by looking at the metrics in more detail – considering what to measure, why, how to measure it, and making sure you are looking at the right data. It is through the analysis and measurement that you'll be able to identify what actions you should be taking if your plan vs actual analysis highlights that something has gone awry.

At the end of this chapter you will have a more detailed understanding as to why planning and controlling will make a difference to your retail business success. Let's get started.

The importance of planning

Investing time in planning will save you money in the long run. For example, buying to a framework based on a well-thought-out plan will mean that you can monitor actual sales performance and take appropriate action to address occasions when actuals don't meet plan. Buying blind will only incur stock issues in future. Of course, planning can never be 100 per cent accurate so it is critical to build flexibility into your business operations in order to allow for the inevitable variances.

A plan allows you to monitor activities in the business compared to that plan. Only the exceptions to the plan, the metrics that deviate from where you wanted them to be, need action to bring them back on track. This is called 'managing by exception'. If things are going to plan, and you've made sure that operationally you can deliver the plan, then you shouldn't need to be making any interventions. If you don't manage by exception then, by default, you will be trying to deal with everything as it happens. This can lead to an overwhelming feeling of being out of control. That's no way to run a business.

The most important reason for having a plan is to enable you to focus your effort on pulling things back on track when necessary.

Another key factor to planning is to have both the high level (often termed the business plan) and the detail (commonly called an operating plan) working together. Let me use an analogy to illustrate this. Imagine you want to go on a long journey to a destination. You know where the destination is, what it is like, and you have a timeline as to when you want to get there. That's a business plan: high-level information; not too much detail. However, no one will be able to help you get to your destination if you don't work out a route map. This will be detailed – you'll know the transport methods, timescales, stops along the way, costs, etc – from this you can work out what you need to do to get to your destination. This is an operating plan: detailed information that you can take action on.

Now at this point you could discover that having done the detailed planning (the route), your business plan (the destination) cannot be reached in the timescale you hoped or for the budget you intended.

Clearly there is a relationship between the two plans – and there will be in your business, too. To continue the analogy, if you want to accelerate the route you may have to invest in more costly transport; does that investment make sense? You will deliver the business plan on time but at higher cost. Alternatively you could keep your route as it is, meaning you deliver the business plan late, but on budget.

Of course, once you start the journey there are also unexpected (exceptional) occurrences – your transport breaks down, the road is blocked – you need to reroute. That's actually where monitoring comes in – making sure you are on plan. When things go off plan, you need to replan according to the destination and resume the journey. This replanning might affect how quickly you reach your destination, or the costs, so a check back to the business plan is very important when any change to the journey is made.

Many people I speak to assume a business plan should include all of the detail; I disagree. It should, however, be reconciled with the detail. Therefore when changes are inevitably made to the detailed operating plan there should always be a check back to the impact that could have on the business plan. If you need to present your business plan to investors or to the bank it should always be backed up with details; perhaps as appendices. Your investors or lenders will certainly want to quiz you on the detail behind some of the high-level statements.

Now you know why you need to have plans in place, let's move on to what the planning elements are and what they should include.

Planning elements

Business plan

We've established that any business should have a business plan. What you intend to do with it will determine how 'polished' it needs to be. The simplest use is for *you*, the business owner. I am not a psychology expert but I do know from experience that when you document your plans, 'externalize' them, and then share them with a trusted third party you will be more committed to delivering on them! I'm sure a psychology expert can explain why; for me it's good enough just to know that it works!

A business plan isn't only the numbers – there needs to be a certain amount of narrative. Much of this narrative is to give you, your team, suppliers, landlord, banks, investors – anyone – a much better understanding of what you are about.

You would start explaining your business with your vision, mission, values, belief, brand, positioning and ideal customer – all the good stuff we covered in Steps 1 to 3. You'd go on to articulate a bit about your product and pricing, channel strategy, customer engagement strategy and supply-chain strategy – all the stuff about *how* you'll deliver on the mission, etc – that's the content from Steps 4 to 8.

This narrative will provide you with a reminder of what your business is all about, who it is for, how it delivers. Very handy if ever you need to refer back to it and validate a decision or a new direction. It should also help to paint a clear picture of your business for any independent third party.

That's all very well and good; but there are no numbers yet, no plan values. That's the next part you need to include.

Overleaf is a simplified example of the content you should be including in your business plan. Some of these will be based on a 'best guess' or estimates from providers, some on the sum of more detailed plans. By using an annual phasing this information is also very valuable to your cash flow.

Note: All figures should be expressed *excluding* VAT – if you want to get really detailed with your cash flow you might want to include a line for VAT; but for the purposes of a high-level business plan, excluding VAT is fine.

I've numbered each item in the table and given an explanation as to what each means, and how to use it, below. If you would rather just download a version in Excel complete with all the formulae, you'll be able to get this from the resources area at **www.retailchampion.co.uk/resources** – it's called 'template business plan'.

So, item by item:

1 Seasonal split of sales per cent – this means what proportion, expressed as a percentage, of the overall planned annual sale will be achieved in each month of the year. This enables you to forecast for seasonality that affects your sales pattern. You can keep it flat such that each month is allocated 1/12th of the year's sale, or increase some months and decrease others in light of how your trading pattern is anticipated.

2 Forecast sales – this is the annual target sales value apportioned to each month using the seasonal split from item 1. Essentially each month sale = annual sale × seasonal factor.

3 Cost of goods is the value in cash of your purchases for resale. Rather than using a margin calculation in the business plan it is better to use an actual budgetary cost-of-goods value as this demonstrates where there are requirements for cash. Retail businesses typically have 'lumpy' cash flow as goods are often purchased for the entire season at the beginning of the season. You need to see this dynamic so you can plan for periods when the business will have a lot of cash flow tied up in stock that is still to be sold.

TABLE 9.1 Business plan template

Item/Month	Jan	Feb	Mar	Apr	May	Jun	Jul	Aug	Sep	Oct	Nov	Dec	YEAR
1 Seasonal split of sales %													
2 Forecast sales £ (based on annual target and seasonal split)													
3 Cost of goods (based on payment due dates for stock orders)													
4 Property costs: rent, rates, service charge, maintenance													
5 Utilities: gas, electric, water, telephone, broadband													
6 Consumables: carrier bags, till rolls, packaging, etc													
7 Salaries and on-costs													
8 IT overheads (hardware, software, hosting, maintenance, support)													

TABLE 9.1 *continued*

Item/Month	Jan	Feb	Mar	Apr	May	Jun	Jul	Aug	Sep	Oct	Nov	Dec	YEAR
9 Marketing and visual merchandising													
10 PR and advertising (including web)													
11 Professional services (business advisor, accountant, lawyer, HR consultant, etc)													
12 Support services (call centre, warehouse operations, book keeping, staff training, etc)													
13 Insurances: property, buildings, content, employers liability, public liability, etc													
14 TOTAL COSTS													
15 TOTAL PROFIT BEFORE TAX													

4   Property costs include the elements of cost associated with your retail premises. If you are in a shopping centre there is often an additional service charge over and beyond the standard rates and rent. Rent can be paid monthly in some cases, but more often is required quarterly, in advance. This is another aspect of the 'lumpy' cash flow, and one that you certainly need to include on the business plan.

5   Utilities will be similar to those you'd have at home, but as a business you usually have the pleasure of paying a much higher rate per unit consumed! These are generally payable monthly.

6   Consumables are all those things that get 'used up' in the course of running the business. From tea and coffee in the staffroom to your carrier bags and packaging. Some consumables, particularly branded carrier bags, may have high minimum order quantities, meaning that this could be another item that you buy infrequently but with a high cost impact during the month you purchase.

7   Salaries and on-costs are all of the costs of employment; payable monthly, and a necessary cost of doing business. You may want to link the salaries to the forecast sales, so if you do have a highly seasonal sales pattern in the business you can plan for increased staffing for your busiest periods.

8   IT overheads will depend on what you have in place; usually you'll be paying for some kind of hardware. You may have purchased it outright and need to depreciate it on your accounts with a budget in your business plan for replacement of old items. You may lease it on a monthly basis. You may be paying for software licences monthly or annually, and you may have a maintenance and support overhead. Whatever the terms, you need to make sure realistic figures are included in the business plan.

9   I've put marketing and visual merchandising together as typically the cost for these aspects can include some design work, some printing and some ongoing maintenance/resource to manage. It would be entirely dependent on your business model as to what you invested. However, it ties in very closely to your marketing and promotional plans. If you are planning a big seasonal event then you should increase the allowance in your budget to accommodate that.

10   PR and advertising, including web, is all about your visibility strategy. You will probably need to allocate a minimum value per month to maintain your position in search, social media and any other media you would want to be seen in. In addition, if you want to draw attention to any big campaign, promotion or event, then you will need to boost the allocation of funds for that in this element of the business plan.

11 Professional services are an all-encompassing title for the skills you would buy in to your business to enable you to either be compliant (eg legal advice on regulations with regard to selling products to the consumer) or to avoid risk (eg legal advice in a lease negotiation) or to develop your business (eg a business advisor to help you define and implement an action plan for growth). Whatever type of service or skill you are buying in, you need to have allowed for it in your costs otherwise you'll find you're making less profit than you forecast!

12 Support services include any part of your business that you could outsource but are subtly different from professional services in that these support services are things you need daily/weekly whereas professional services might be less frequent: ad hoc or quarterly, for example. You should allocate a minimum monthly budget for these services. If any of the costs are proportional to sales you may also want to link the costs to the sales, in the same way you did with staffing.

13 Insurance – we all know what that means! Depending on your lease you may or may not need to include buildings insurance. You should speak to a credible broker and get cover that's suitable without going too far. Don't cut corners on insurance, though; you'll be very glad of it if and when you need it. Typically it can be paid monthly although that may increase the total cost per annum.

14 This is the total of all of the costs – the sum of all values from items 3 to 13. It will be an estimate based on the best available information. It should vary each month (as costs will vary) and it should include all fixed and variable overheads: your costs of doing business.

15 This is the best line – the profit before tax. Essentially this is the difference between item 2 and item 14. In some months you might see a negative value – that's where you need cash flow to support you. In other months you will see a positive value – that's cash flow you need to save to support negative months. Over the whole year you *must* see a positive value; and one that is representative of all the time and effort you invest in running your business. That's *your* income. You can choose to draw a salary (and include that in item 7) or you can choose to draw earnings from the profit line. Either way, that profit line is what you want to replicate, with your robust and repeatable processes, to achieve that scalable, saleable business.

Now you know what needs to be in a business plan. Of course, it is how you then use it that really counts.

Once you've got the high-level figures you need to start looking at your detailed plans. You need to make sure these align with, and support the achievement of, your high-level plan. If the figures don't match you need to address the difference. Obviously if the difference is a minor per cent variation then you can ignore it; after all, this is only a plan. If the difference is more than say 10 to 15 per cent then you should look at how to address it. You could either re-phase the high-level plan or revise the detailed plan, whichever seems more realistic and achievable.

Next I'd consider having a version of the business plan for each of your channels and locations – so you can monitor sales and costs for each outlet and channel. Using the same template, but at channel and location level, means that as your business grows you will be able to identify those which are underperforming compared to others. Knowing which stores or channels are problematic enables you to drill down into the reasons why so that you can fix the issues before they start to become a drain on the rest of the business.

Finally, and possibly one of the most important uses of your business plan, is to seek funding or to prove your credibility to a landlord.

I'll start by talking about landlords. It may come as a surprise, given that numerous reports are telling us that there is a surplus of vacant retail premises, to learn landlords are very choosy about who they lease their premises to. In a challenging market, landlords don't want to get a short-term letting only to see their tenant fail. The disruption to them is significant; they have to bear the cost of reletting and the renegotiation of the lease. In addition, if a series of businesses fail in a location then the location itself gets a bad name. Not good if the landlord wants to sell their property in the near future. The outcome is that landlords are increasingly cautious about who they will take on as the leaseholder for their premises. They want a long-term tenant who will become established, who will take care of their property, and who will be able to meet their financial obligations under the terms of the lease.

Your business plan will make a difference to a picky landlord. When Sarah Decent wanted to open a new Modish store in Cambridge she had to present her case to the landlords, who enjoyed some of the lowest vacancy rates in the UK. Why should they let a small retail brand trade from their store? How could this brand prove it was not a risk but a good choice as a tenant? The answer was in an elegant pack Sarah pulled together for them. It included all of the business plan narrative, lots of images, a couple of the high-level plan values (business growth targets and trading forecasts), and appendices about her credibility as a local businesswoman – press cuttings, references and awards. This pack made the difference. We know it did; they told us!

The other reason for your business plan to make a public outing is if you are seeking financial support. Whether that is a loan or overdraft from your bank, or an investment from a VC or private 'business angel', the single most important document will be your business plan.

Slightly different from the detail Sarah presented to the landlords, this version of the plan needs all the figures. The narrative should still be included to 'paint the picture'; appendices (where you have them) should be included to add to your credibility, and the detailed figures *must* stack up because that's how the financiers will determine if they believe you will be able to meet your financial obligations to them. Investors will additionally want to understand how your business will provide them with a good return on their investment.

Once you have the initial interest of a bank or an investor they will want to do a 'due diligence' process and go through your business with a fine-tooth comb. You will inevitably be asked to provide *all* the detail that demonstrates how, operationally, your business will be able to achieve the figures in the business plan. This is the linkage between your business plan and all of the more detailed planning aspects; so we'll start to look at those now.

Operating plan

Your detailed operating plan can be used to manage and monitor your business performance on a daily/weekly basis. It enables you to keep track of sales, stock, overheads and cash flow.

Much of this you already should have the ingredients for – the range plan is key; and you also have a marketing and promotional plan. One aspect that is very powerful which we have not yet covered in detail is WSSI – this stands for 'weekly sales, stock and intake planning'. Used by retailers large and small, it began life as a planning and controlling tool in the 1980s in Burton Retail Group in London. WSSI enables you to create a rolling stock flow based on forecast sales and to identify when additional stock will be required to support sales.

Using the range plan to build WSSI, a stock plan and a cash flow

For a smaller retailer WSSI is a good tool to use to keep tabs on sales, stock and intake (receipts of stock).

Below is a really simple view of a WSSI. As this is classically managed at style – colour level (the level that you would calculate the order quantity for) then even if you only have 500 items offered for sale it's a lot of work to manage if you are doing it manually, on a spreadsheet. With that in mind don't try to dive into too much detail; you don't want it to stop adding value and become just an administrative exercise.

By taking each line from the range plan, start with the average weekly rate of sale in units. If you know your seasonality you can apply a seasonal factor, and obviously that helps to calculate a more accurate stock flow. Then you should roll the WSSI forward for a full season, typically 26 weeks, longer if you sell continuity lines. There is an example overleaf. If you want to download a template WSSI, including formulae, visit **www.retailchampion.co.uk/resources** – it's called 'template WSSI'.

TABLE 9.2 Weekly sales, stock and intake plan (WSSI) template

Item [description of item]	Week 1	Week 2	Week 3	Week 4
Seasonal factor (multiplier of average weekly rate of sale)	1.2	1.3	1.1	0.9
Sales forecast (units) Ave rate of sale = 10pw	12	13	11	9
Opening stock	20	18	15	14
Intake	10	10	10	10
Closing stock	18	15	14	15

The above example shows how you can develop a simple WSSI. If you don't have a weekly intake of stock, purchasing larger upfront quantities, a WSSI can highlight when you will be out of stock of an item, assuming sales track to forecast.

TABLE 9.3 Using your WSSI to help identify potential future stock issues

Item [description of item]	Week 1	Week 2	Week 3	Week 4
Seasonal factor (multiplier of average weekly rate of sale)	1.2	1.3	1.1	0.9
Sales forecast (units) Ave = 10	12	13	11	9
Opening stock	40	28	15	4
Intake	0	0	0	0
Closing stock	28	15	4	–5

In the highlighted column your WSSI would have shown you that the initial intake (opening stock) of 40 units was insufficient to meet the forecast sales.

It would alert you to either increase the initial order quantity or to bring in a replenishment order at week three.

This is very simplified but hopefully illustrates how you might use the data from the range plan to create a WSSI.

If you want to apply a seasonal factor you can do this by looking at past sales performance for a period of time. Calculate the average rate of sale for that period and divide the actual sales in any given week by the average. The answer you get is the factor that you would apply to your planned rate of sale to get to a rough seasonality estimate.

The following example illustrates this.

Step 1 – look at historical data and calculate the average rate of sale for the period.

TABLE 9.4 To calculate a seasonal factor, firstly review historical sales data

Past wks	Wk1	Wk2	Wk3	Wk4	Wk5	Wk6	Wk7	Wk8	TOTAL
Sales	10	11	13	9	8	9	10	12	82

The average weekly rate of sale for the period is 82/8 = 10.25.

Step 2 – Divide the rate of sale per week by the average to determine the seasonal factors.

TABLE 9.5 Using the historical sales data, determine a seasonal factor by each sales period

Planned wks	Wk1	Wk2	Wk3	Wk4	Wk5	Wk6	Wk7	Wk8
Factor	0.98	1.07	1.27	0.88	0.78	0.88	0.98	1.17

Step 3 is to multiply your estimated forecast rate of sale by the factors and there you have it: your weekly sales forecast with some seasonality considered. There is a 'template seasonal factor calculation' in the resources area via **www.retailchampion.co.uk/resources**.

This approach gives you a better weekly sales profile than if you used a flat rate of sale value across all of the sales periods. You will then see the

WSSI produce a much more accurate stock-flow plan. If you overlay any planned promotions or events, to account for any further expected increase in sales, it becomes more accurate again.

Using the intake line from your WSSI you also now have a clear stock-flow plan. Apply the cost price of that item to that stock-flow plan and you have a clear cost of stock per week/period which will effectively impact your more detailed cash flow. This is also key data that need to be cross-checked against the business plan; but it's not that difficult to derive once you have your WSSI in place. Similarly, using the sales units line from your WSSI and applying the retail price will give you a clear view of cash sales forecast.

WSSI is very powerful – you'll have all the data at your fingertips, now it's just a case of using it!

Much of the data from WSSI can feed into a cash flow plan. That's what we'll look at next.

Cash flow plan

Your cash-flow plan should be considerably more detailed than your business plan. It should show all income and all expenditure, ideally by week, in order that you can make sure you continue to be able to pay your bills. If you plan your cash carefully, and notice that something might tip you into difficulties at a future point, you are at least in a position to speak to your supplier or your landlord about the issue and perhaps agree that you'll pay a smaller amount in your difficult month and make up the difference in the following month.

Many profitable businesses have failed because they hadn't got cash to meet their contractual obligations. A business with no cash cannot trade. You can, however, get through a few difficult months if you are open and honest with those who you need to be paying – most will agree that they'd rather get paid late than not at all. A cash-flow plan enables you to have these conversations *before* it becomes too serious.

Be as detailed as you can with cash flow – for instance, where the business plan did not include VAT, the cash flow should. In the period from VAT return to VAT return you will be accruing VAT owed in your bank; when the VAT period ends you need to pay that VAT. Having the accruing VAT on hand in the bank is a bonus for a temporary cash-flow boost; but you have to be able to pay it out again when the time comes.

To do your cash flow you should take the rows from the business plan and expand them out – itemize everything you can, eg instead of utilities have a row each for water, gas, electric, phones and broadband. Use your bank statements to identify when payments are due (which week of each month) and how much typically is due. It may seem onerous, but if you have a good forward view of cash flow then you're going to be in a much stronger position – both in terms of your confidence to invest in things that deliver value to your business and in terms of getting through future difficulties because you can see them coming, and you can plan for them.

As your cash flow plan is going to depend on how you trade I'm not going to create a template – the business plan is a great starting point and you can build something specific to your business from that.

The next area to consider is not relevant to all retailers, but as it has a significant impact on a fairly sizeable group it's worthy of mention.

Ratio planning for fashion; or any product areas with a size mix

I wanted to just give a moment to fashion retailers, who do have one other consideration to make in their planning that other retailers don't.

A number of my clients are involved in various fashion-related businesses – from menswear to lingerie to shoes. I often find myself having conversations with those who I'd generically term 'fashion retailers' as they have a common issue – that's the ability to sell through on *all* the sizes that they need to order to complete their range. While a common issue for fashion retailers, *any* retailer who has a selection of sizes within a product range could be affected by this; and that's the importance of ratio planning.

Getting the size ratios right is a key factor in profitable fashion retailing. When working on the range plan we're generally considering the style – colour level of detail – we understand, for example, what the likely rate of sale is going to be for a pair of navy cotton chino trousers compared to a beige pair or to a pair of khaki linen drawstring trousers. We know this from past experience, supplier insights, observed trends and, it is fair to say, a bit of guesswork.

This estimated average weekly rate of sale can thus determine what the seasonal buy quantity for each style – colour combination should be. That would be fine if we were planning almost anything other than fashion. We'd send the order to the approved supplier and the delivery would arrive at the agreed destination at some point in future.

With fashion, though, we have to break down the order at style – colour into a size split so that the manufacturer can provide the range of sizes we want to present to the customers.

Getting this right at the point of order will impact the entire performance, and ultimately profitability, of the product.

When you think about it, it's obvious. Consumers buy at SKU level – that is the absolute item – a style, colour, size combination. Depending on the garment, colours, shape, how fashionable it is, your branding, etc, you will attract different customers of different sizes to different ranges, styles and even different colours.

Keeping track of your past sales performance by SKU will enable you to analyse your ideal future ratios. You don't want to overcomplicate things and get into too much detail, so try to avoid using too many different ratios. Planning your ratios at range level is likely to be adequate, but if there are key styles where it will impact on your profitability if you *don't* have a style-specific ratio then, by exception, plan the ratio at style level.

TABLE 9.6 Size ratio calculation template

Size	Seasonal sales (units)	Size ratio (%)
12 S	20	10
12 M	25	12.5
12 L	10	5
14 S	15	7.5
14 M	40	20
14 L	20	10
16 S	10	5
16 M	35	17.5
16 L	25	10
TOTAL	200	100

Here is an example based on a range of ladies trousers offered in UK sizes 12–16 and leg length short, medium and long. Beware: if you sell out of a size early on you will never see it reach its potential. Ensure you base your ratio analysis on a period when you had plenty of stock of all sizes!

There is a 'template size ratio calculation' in the resources area – **www.retailchampion.co.uk/resources**.

The fact is that if you don't buy enough of a popular size you will sell out and lose potential sales. If you buy too many of a less popular size you will have excess stock that remain long after the popular sizes have all gone.

In the end you have only two choices to clear the stock:

1 Place a specific order for just the popular sizes to bring the product 'back into ratio' and continue the line, possibly carrying forward to the next season to enable full-price sell-through (better for profitability, but not ideal if the product doesn't 'belong' alongside your carefully planned next season range).

2 Reduce the stock that hasn't sold – thus losing margin to fund the clearance activity.

Not ideal as all of this simply adds workload to implement actions to deal with a problem that could have been avoided had your size ratio been more accurate at the point of order.

If you have an EPOS system then you can analyse your sales by size to get a much better view of the size ratio to order at the next buying point. If you don't yet trade, or don't have EPOS, it will be more difficult, but not impossible. If you do sufficient research, ask people such as your suppliers as well as your future customers, you'll get a clearer view as to what size ratio you need to best service your customer demand.

Relevance of EPOS

I mentioned EPOS above. In my view any serious retailer these days needs to have an EPOS system – not only does it help you analyse performance, track stock and speed up the sales process, but it holds key data: everything you need to understand your sales at the lowest level of detail. A good EPOS holds receipt-level data and with this you can discover anything and everything about your business... at least if you know what reports you need, and how to analyse them. Using EPOS effectively will unlock so much potential from your retail business; and you'll have answers to all these questions at the push of a button:

- How many transactions do I make per day?
- What's the average transaction value?
- Are some items regularly bought together?
- What do my sales tell me about my size ratios?

EPOS is a critical tool and one that will get mentioned a good deal more before the end of this book!

EPOS can also be fundamental to the ability to report on actuals, and thus when combined with the data from your plans will provide you with powerful analytics; which we'll come on to next.

Analytics: measurement, reporting and controlling

There isn't much point in having all these plans if you're not going to use them to compare them with your actual business performance. You'll only achieve your targets if you drive the business forward and constantly keep an eye on plan vs actual.

To do this we need data on your actual performance. I mentioned EPOS above – if you have EPOS your actuals are probably just a touch of a button away. If you don't have one yet, put 'Get an EPOS system implemented' as a high-priority item on your action plan. In the absence of EPOS you should track the data you can as best you can. Then, instead of investing a considerable amount of your time trying to get to the detail, invest that time more wisely by getting your EPOS in place asap! I can't advocate any retail business owner trying to do the analytics of their business performance (sales, stock, costs and cash flow) in any level of detail if they can't extract the data from an EPOS. It will take you so much time to do it manually that it won't be worth it – you have a business to run! EPOS is an investment in your robust, repeatable processes and systems. When you have it in place you will be able to do all of these steps much more efficiently.

What key data about actual performance do we need, and why?

Well it depends what questions you want to ask of your business. If you want to understand your ratios for forward planning a fashion purchase then you would look at the mix of sizes sold across a range of products for a given period of time. For most EPOS systems this is a simple report.

If you want to understand what items are most commonly purchased with another item, then again that would be a simple EPOS report of all transactions containing the primary product over a given time frame. You could then look at the frequency that other items appeared alongside.

If you want to understand average transaction value on each day of the week, perhaps to compare performance of weekend sales staff to those working in the week, you could look at a report for average transaction value per day and determine which days had achieved the best average transaction value. You could map that to which team members were working on those days and begin to correlate better sales with certain staff... the options for finding insights into your business performance from your data are endless! The trick is not to get caught up in the detail but to focus on what matters to your business, what information would help you to identify areas where can you improve, and where opportunities lie.

Right now, though, we're looking at measuring your actual trading performance compared to your plan. You need to be able to notice when things are not going to plan and to take action accordingly. To do this you ideally need to report on weekly unit sales by item – this can then be compared to WSSI so that you can make sure that sales are tracking forecast. For the items where things are not going to plan, the exceptions, you can put in place actions to mitigate the risk of having overstocks or sell-outs. The plan vs actual report gives you forewarning of issues that would otherwise be potentially damaging to your business. If you're measuring plan vs actual, and your competition aren't, I know who'll be more profitable!

It isn't only the WSSI data you should be tracking. You should also be looking at planned values vs actuals for *all* of the rows of the business plan.

Where you have derived the sales line in cash value make sure you check the achieved sales vs the planned sales each month and what impact that has. On your detailed cash flow plan you should make sure you're recording your actual income and expenditure on a weekly basis so as to avoid any nasty surprises. You can do this by recording the actual values of expenditure from your bank statements or from your accounting system and your actual sales values can come from your EPOS data. Of course, if you're a whizz on a spreadsheet you can always set up formulae on your business plan so that it automatically updates with the actual values based on the sum of the values from the detailed cash flow. This would mean you only need to input the actual values on one sheet so it will save you time.

The crux of all of this is to make sure that your business performance is tracking along to plan. You need to be checking that the actual figures reported aren't going to be an issue for you and that you will still be able to meet your commitments and targets. If there does appear to be deviation from plan that causes you concern, then you can address it as soon as it is identified in order to avoid a problem compounding and spiralling out of control.

Once you've got the processes and tools in place it should only take a couple of hours each week to input the actual values and review the results. What you learn about your business, the confidence this kind of analytics gives you in your decision making, will really make a difference to how you run your business. There is only one thing you really should be aware of, an issue I've seen on several occasions... when you are analysing the business performance you need to make sure you are considering *all* the details, that *all* the data you need to base your decisions on have been captured. If you don't, you risk drawing incorrect conclusions from the data. I wanted to touch on this before closing this chapter.

Importance of using the right metrics

When it comes to metrics you need to know what you are measuring, why, how to measure, and be certain that you are looking at the right data. It may sound obvious, but let me give you a classic example of how this can go badly wrong. This comes from a mid-sized (c. 50 outlets) luxury retailer who sells toiletries and cosmetics. This retailer was keen to understand their profit return on space. They had the following data available:

- units of space per store;
- sales per store;
- average sales margin.

Using this alone the retailer determined the sales per unit of space per store and derived an average margin per unit of space per store. They thought they had the answer, a spread of performance across the chain and identifiable top and bottom performers. Rural stores were at the bottom (making least sales, thus least margin, per unit of space), city stores were at the top (with greatest sales, thus greatest margin, per unit of space). But this was *not* the metric they should have been looking at. The requirement was to understand *profit* return on space. Let's assume that more or less all of the costs of sales were equal – staffing to make the sales, running costs of the stores (utilities, etc) – therefore in a rough analysis there is one major variable that would influence the spread of performance across the chain – the property cost.

When the cost per unit of space per store was considered in the metric, suddenly the spread was very different. As the rental cost for a rural store was typically a fraction of the rental for a city-centre store it became apparent that rural stores were strong contributors to the profitability of the chain, in fact, in many cases their profitability exceeded that of the higher-sales-volume city stores.

This story illustrates the risk of not understanding the metrics when doing performance analysis. That particular retailer might have considered closing its lowest-performing stores, and had they have taken the initial analysis as an accurate picture they'd have certainly closed some of the stores that actually contributed to the profit line quite significantly!

Linked to using the right metrics is also using the tools correctly, and making sure that the data input is accurate. There is a saying when it comes to data and analytics: 'rubbish in, rubbish out'. If you input the data incorrectly in the first place you don't stand a chance of getting the right answers when it comes to analysis. That's another reason why I am an advocate of effective tools such as EPOS. Apart from setting it up with new products and prices, thereon in the system does the recording; you can define the reporting, and hey presto, everything else is done for you. The room for error is considerably reduced.

In the next chapter, Step 10, back office, we'll look in more detail at EPOS as the core IT investment for any serious retailer.

Summing up

Well, that's as much as we really need to cover to give you a good start on Step 9 – planning and controlling. Congratulations – there is only one more step to go and you'll have completed the 10 steps to retail success!

To recap what we have covered in this chapter: it was all about effective planning, from the high-level business plan down to the detailed stock-flow and cash-flow plan. The purpose? To enable you, the business owner, to make confident, commercially sound decisions.

We talked about the importance of planning, and how that enables you to 'manage by exception' – focusing only on the areas where things were not going to plan.

We've then looked at a high-level business plan and a detailed operating plan. We used an analogy that the high-level plan is all about the destination whereas the detailed operating plan is about the journey to get there. In this section we looked in more detail at planning elements such as WSSI, which feeds stock flow and cash flow, and which would be used to monitor sales and stock on a weekly basis. Alongside the detailed planning we also had a brief look at ratio planning, which is most applicable to fashion retailers.

Finally we looked at the relevance of analytics – comparing your plans to actual performance. I highlighted that if you want to be able to better control your business, to track actual performance, it would be wise to invest in the appropriate tools and technology – eg EPOS. In the last part of this chapter we discussed the importance of using the right metrics, and making sure that the measurement was accurate, in order to confidently take decisions that affect your business.

So now you should feel quite clear as to what you need to be doing to embed more rigour around your planning and controlling processes. We're now ready to move onto the final step: Step 10 – back office.

Chapter Ten
Back office

Introduction

This is Step 10, back office, the last of them all! I don't want to bore you with all the nitty-gritty, non-product, non-customer-facing 'stuff', *but* how you manage the back office of your business will be one of your enablers for growth.

In this chapter we're going to take a look at the aspects of business that are more about 'keeping things ticking over' than about delivering direct commercial impact – but don't assume these are not important – if you don't get this stuff right a considerable amount of your time will be consumed sorting it all out; so focus on getting the back office working effectively and you'll find out that you're not tied up with these tasks, free to focus on the growth plans.

We're going to look at four areas, non-core to your retail operations, which play a hugely important role. We'll review why each is important and why you should include all four when planning your business:

1 Human Resources: we'll look at how you plan your organization, roles, responsibilities, skills, knowledge, recruitment, training, policies, etc.

2 Legal: looking at the part a good legal representative can play in regulatory considerations, contractual negotiations, protection of your brand and intellectual property rights.

3 Finance: beyond managing your cash, this includes accounting, risk management, audit and compliance.

4 IT: we'll consider all of the different types of business systems we've mentioned throughout the book, how these can be deployed, and what you need to be considering when it comes to selecting solutions for such things as EPOS, e-commerce, and CRM.

Finally, we'll look at how you could go about including these functions in your business now and in the future, considering outsourcing vs in-house.

At the end of this chapter you'll have a good understanding of the important role each of these four back-office functions can play in your business.

As this is the last step, let's get going!

Human Resources

Your organization, and by this I mean the people within it and the roles and responsibilities they have, delivers your business plan. The people you recruit, their abilities, knowledge, skills, attitudes, values and behaviours all affect *your* ability to meet your promises to your customers. The policies you implement, the processes you operate by, the systems that provide your information flow, and the training you provide on all of these areas then affect *their* ability to meet your promises to your customers. The good news is that this doesn't all have to be done by you; the majority can be done by an HR expert (with your input, of course).

In a larger organization the purpose of a good HR function would be to deliver all of these activities, reporting to the board. A major corporate would have a team of people in an HR function doing organizational design and resource planning; recruitment, induction and training; salary budgeting; and reward planning. They would implement all core business policies and undertake all performance management activities. Indeed, in a big retail organization that team of people in the HR department looks after one of the top three costs for the business (people; where product and property are the other two most significant costs). As a smaller business, or if you are just starting out and as yet only planning for growth, be mindful of this. People are one of your top three costs, therefore it goes without saying that you need to treat the management of the people, the human resource, as seriously as you would the purchasing of stock or the signing of a lease on a property! Of course, you're unlikely to need a whole HR department for some time, so it would probably make sense to find an individual to help you: a freelance HR expert or consultant. Ideally, in the early days you need an HR expert who can work with you on an hourly charged basis so you get high-quality input but only what you need.

At this point it is probably worth mentioning that I am a strong believer in achieving success by surrounding yourself with experts. In this instance we're talking about an HR expert specifically. I do believe, however, that if you are serious about growing your business (and if you've read this far I will assume that you are), you should be looking to find the very best people you can afford to work with to plug any skills and knowledge gaps you may have, or to help you replicate your precious time; it will be worthwhile. As a business owner you can't be expected to be brilliant at everything. In fact you don't actually need to be an expert in anything! Successful business owners rarely are experts, unless their business is based on their unique expertise (like mine is). Think about it just for a moment. We said it before in Chapter 7: Richard Branson probably doesn't know how to pilot his aeroplanes and Bill Gates probably can't write lines of programme code for the latest version of Windows (although he did come from a technical background).

As a business owner what you need to be great at is the overview, driving your business forward with your strategy and vision, your management and motivation. Bringing in experts to get things done right, first time, to a very high standard, will stand you in good stead for your future growth.

You may be thinking, 'We're supposed to be talking about HR right now' – well, in fact we are. If you *do* choose to bring expert support into your business from time to time you would be wise to involve your HR advisor in the selection process. The HR advisor will help you to clarify their role and responsibilities and also assess if they are a good fit for your existing team. Even though someone is only going to be working with you part-time, or on a temporary basis, you still need to know that they will fit in with your existing team and a be a good match to your values and culture.

Now, focusing back onto the core activities you might want to hand over to an HR expert, the list below should give you some ideas as to the scope of help and advice a good HR person could provide, and if you are selecting someone to support you with your HR requirements you could use this as the basis for your 'checklist'.

Check whether the HR expert is able to support with the following:

- Organizational design: could you sit down with this person, explain your business plan and vision, and work out the organizational structure for the short, mid and long term?

- Roles and responsibilities: could you then drill down from the high-level organizational design to determine the roles that each functional area would undertake, where the responsibilities were assigned, and where the responsibilities were handed over from one functional area to another?

- Job design: can the HR expert develop job roles based on the planned organization? Can they develop a skills matrix for each job that would make advertising, selection and recruitment of resources easier?

- Recruitment process: can the HR expert identify the ideal routes for recruitment, eg advertising through agencies, headhunters, job centres, colleges, apprenticeship schemes, etc? Can the HR expert undertake initial screening of CVs compared to job specifications and skills matrices to shortlist suitable candidates for interview?

- Interview process: can the HR expert develop an interview process that limits the impact on *your* time but ensures a consistent, standard approach to assessment of candidates?

- Selection and appointment of staff: can the HR expert support you in the decision making regarding the appointment of new resources based on the interview outcomes? Can they provide you with all necessary and appropriate templates to comply with employment law in terms of offer letters, contracts of employment, company handbooks/policies/guidelines, etc?

- Implementation of appropriate HR policies: can the HR expert ensure you have all the relevant policies in place for protection of your business, your staff and yourself; to ensure compliance with all legal obligations surrounding employment law?

- Training design: does your HR expert have knowledge in your industry sector? Will they be competent in putting together induction packs and training for new starters?

- Employee development and performance management: can the HR expert support you in ongoing development and performance management of your team? Can they help with performance reviews and succession planning? Are they confident in dealing with poor performers?

- Handling staff issues: can the HR expert support you in dealing with staff issues such as absenteeism, unreliability and any other issues in the workplace? Can they support you if there is ever a grievance brought against you by a member of staff? Would the HR expert have the skills and abilities to represent you in an employment tribunal or litigious situation?

I am sure you can add to this list. The list alone should remind you just how important it will be to have a robust set of HR practices, policies, processes and documents in order to protect you, your business and your staff from any issues that could arise, especially as your business grows and takes on more employees.

As I mentioned litigation in the last point it seems appropriate to now move on to consider the important role a legal representative can play in your business.

Legal

Having a good legal advisor is like buying insurance – they only prove their value when things go wrong. Legal advice is costly; although usually you do get what you pay for. Professional practices have 'indemnity insurance' – this means you are protected by their insurers if the advice they give you is proven to have been detrimental to you. It is always worth going through the official routes as opposed to 'having a friend who is a lawyer check it over' – there will be no comeback on that sort of arrangement, and chances are if things go wrong you'll be losing a friend as well as a whole lot more!

There are three general areas where a smaller retail business should be considering getting legal advice. These include:

- Regulatory considerations: such as remote-selling legislation for e-commerce, consumer-rights legislation for in-store, credit legislation if you offer credit terms or accept credit card payments.

- Contractual negotiations: such as lease negotiations, product supply contracts and any capital purchases such as IT systems or a building contract for a major refit of your store.

- Protection of your brand and intellectual property rights: you might choose to trademark your brand, you may have specific products that you design and develop for which you should own the design rights, you may have content on your website or in your brochure for which you should own copyright.

Typically, lawyers are highly expert in a very narrow field. You may find a single practice has a specialist retail team, in which case they should have capabilities across all of the above three areas. You may need to be speaking to two different practices – one specializing in brand protection and intellectual property, one in the more contractual side of things, usually termed 'commercial contract law'.

My advice would be to speak to a few different lawyers before you choose who to work with. Get a feel for how you could work with them: Do you like the person? Did you feel they understood your business and your needs? Get some examples of past client work, testimonials, and evidence of their skill in your specific sector and for your specific requirements. Check that you will have a dedicated person who will be your point of contact; you don't want to have the initial conversation with someone you like only to find that you are always filtered through a secretary or assistant, never speaking to the person representing you. Check that you will be able to call or e-mail and ask a question without incurring a bill for every minute you might consume. This is an area that often catches people by surprise – if you don't check the terms of business in real detail you might discover that what you thought was a simple e-mail exchange to clarify something has cost you 30 minutes of their charge-out rate! You need to be crystal clear about how they make their charges before you appoint them.

My advice is that you need to check everything when it comes to choosing a lawyer – mistakes can be very expensive. Only when you are absolutely confident that they can not only meet your requirements but also operate a business model that you are comfortable with should you appoint them. As a non-legal expert you won't know what 'good' looks like – this is why seeking some recommendations from their other clients, ideally smaller retailers like you, will be invaluable.

That's all I plan to cover on legal aspects – I don't think for a minute you'd imagine *any* business should operate without having some form of legal advice at some time or other. As a retailer, considering that property and product are two of your top three cost drivers, getting your contracts right and favourable is something your lawyer will do for you, and that's why they're such an important ingredient for the management of your back office.

Next we'll look at the importance of finance as a back-office function.

Finance

In the last chapter I talked about the importance for you, as the business owner, to keep a close eye on your cash-flow management. Even when you've grown, and are CEO of your multi-million-pound retail empire, I'd still expect you to be having regular updates with your finance director and there is no doubt that cash flow would be on your agenda. However, as a function, finance is far wider than just the management of cash; there are statutory and regulatory obligations to meet. In the UK these include reporting to HMRC (Her Majesty's Revenue and Customs) and to Companies House. The specifics of what you have to do will depend on the size of your business, your business structure, and what trading activities you undertake. You should speak to an accountant to ascertain what your specific statutory duties and obligations include. There are significant penalties for company directors who fail to meet their statutory obligations; these include heavy fines and can include imprisonment. Finance is, then, I am sure you'd agree, of critical importance as a back-office function – the risks to you personally, and to your business, can be catastrophic if you don't adhere to the regulations.

In addition to ensuring you are compliant and meet all your deadlines a good finance function would contribute to your business planning, budgeting, cash-flow management, securing funding, as well as helping you assess and manage your business risk, and auditing processes for efficiency and cost savings. In the early days it would probably be prudent to consider working with an hourly-paid contract commercial finance manager on similar terms to your HR expert. As your business grows it would make sense to recruit someone to work alongside you as a finance manager to really support you in what will be a key function to underpin the success of your business.

Alongside a finance expert working with you in the business you will also need to consider appointing an accountancy practice. You aren't obliged to have an accountant to review your statutory submissions but it is wise to do so. They can check everything is in order as well as identify things you might have missed – often areas where you can make taxation savings – so they can earn back the cost of their fees by identification of legitimate tax savings. Some accountancy practices can additionally offer you bookkeeping resources. You may find that one of your staff can do your bookkeeping; or you may want to outsource that. As long as it is done accurately and recorded in a manner that can easily be integrated into your accounts it doesn't matter what you choose to do – they key is to keep on top of it all and make sure it gets done.

To sum up on finance: there are various activities that you need to make sure are completed, on time and accurately, to meet your statutory obligations. There are various other ways in which a finance expert could support your business – it all depends on what you need. Bookkeeping? Accountancy? Commercial finance expertise? Assess how you can resource for those needs – maybe that's a mix of in-house resource, contracted resource or outsourcing to an accountancy practice. Select who you work with in much the same way as you did with the HR expert and the legal practice – by understanding their capabilities, expertise and charging model.

A good back office needs a good finance infrastructure. Designing how yours operates might be a task for you and your HR expert to work on together. In addition, finance depends on the availability of accurate data, information, reports and analytics. Well, that's the responsibility of the fourth area of back office: IT.

IT

Where would we be without access to IT these days? If you think you can run a modern, successful business without a significant use of, and dependency on, Information Technology, think again. IT enables the recording and transmission of data and transactions, the automation of processes and the access to reporting and analytics that would otherwise take an eternity to reproduce on paper. It also enables the sharing of information with a variety of third parties and connects all of the 'actors' in the extended supply chain – from supply of goods to sale to customer.

There are three main areas to consider when it comes to IT:

- Hardware: if you are ever confused about what hardware is, a friend of mine once said 'Hardware is the part of the system that you can kick' – and you may often want to! Hardware is the physical machinery that the software (the stuff you can't kick) runs on.

- Infrastructure: the connectivity – cables, servers, broadband, cloud, hosting... all the stuff that enables data and information to pass from a user on one device to another user on a different device, often in a different place.

- Software: the programs that run on your hardware; the visible user interface that you interact with; the coding that connects you and your screen with data (words, images, video) stored in a database. Even Internet Explorer or Google Chrome is software; although you might not have thought of it that way before!

You need all three of these IT elements in your business.

Typically, what hardware you have is in part a matter of choice, in part a necessity based on the activities you want to undertake. For example, you will need a credit card machine and receipt printer if you want to take credit card transactions. You probably also need a PC; but it's up to you if you prefer a laptop or a desktop. Some software may require minimum specification levels for your hardware – your software provider will need to ensure you know the details.

Infrastructure may also be dictated by the software you choose – so you'll need to specify the requirements for this when you understand how you need to implement your software. Infrastructure needs to be reliable, so it's worth having some kind of IT support service in place to make sure that you don't lose your connections to the rest of the world.

Software is the big one. I've worked for SAP, one of the world's largest software companies and also Accenture, one of the biggest consultancies and systems integrators on the planet. I've seen literally millions of £/$ wasted on software implementations. If I could distil all the reasons why IT implementations have failed to deliver benefit for organizations into one single message of advice it would be: **Start with the end in mind**. What I mean by this is that when you start thinking about your requirements you should have a vision of the future processes and operating model in mind. You should define the requirements for your business systems based on that future model, not on the here and now. What tools are going to be needed by which business functions to support which processes? Are you thinking a good five to seven years forward? Don't fall into the trap of just fixing a need today with something that will 'do for now'. The most successful software implementations make a concerted effort to do it once, and do it right. Obviously technology and business process requirements move on, so upgrades to your software will be essential. However, if you can justify the cost of building your systems such that they are as future-proofed as possible then you will absolutely be platformed for growth.

There will be times when you simply can't afford to go for the ideal future-proof solution. That's fine. Put it in the business plan, allocate funds, and do it as soon as you can. In the meantime do what you need to do. If that means buying into software knowing full well that it will be replaced in two to three years' time, then do it. You can plan for the depreciation of the investment, it will do its job in the interim period, and it is a step in the right direction, a step towards your end game.

Throughout this book I've mentioned various business processes that are typically enabled by software. While we can't appraise all the options here I'd like to recap on those so you have a view as to what ingredients you may want to consider in your IT infrastructure, and why.

My advice is to reflect on any notes you've made about IT and systems throughout all of the preceding steps. You need to consider which software systems might really accelerate your ability to do specific actions in your business. From this you need to determine what you need to be considering in terms of your business systems implementation plan. It is certainly worth getting some expert advice, sitting down together, reviewing your business plan and areas for focus vs the 10 steps to retail success and the IT opportunities you have identified. From this you can design what your system landscape needs to be in the future. You need to plan how you will get there in a step-by-step way, which won't break the bank, which won't be too much change for you to embed with your teams all at once, but which will achieve your goal in the most efficient manner.

TABLE 10.1 Which software/systems can support retail business process, and why a retailer should consider using such software/systems

Software solution type	Business processes supported	Why you should consider it
EPOS	Recording transactions; set-up of products, pricing and promotions. Holds stock records and provides real-time stock availability. Usually includes a full suite of hourly, daily, weekly, monthly reports on sales, stock, margin, transaction value, number of transactions. The data from EPOS underpin almost all analytics for performance management and planning.	With EPOS it's more a case of how can you operate effectively without it! EPOS has come up in several of the steps we have covered. Given the number of business processes it can support it should be your top priority project if you aren't already using it.
E-commerce	Presenting products for sale via the internet, taking transactions online. If you are retailing in-store as well as online a good e-commerce should ideally feed from all of the data within EPOS. If you only retail online then your e-commerce database needs to incorporate all of the capability of an EPOS system.	If you plan to retail via the internet you need an e-commerce solution. Unlike EPOS there really is no manual alternative. Remote selling requires that customers can complete a transaction with no human interaction.

TABLE 10.1   *continued*

Software solution type	Business processes supported	Why you should consider it
CRM and loyalty	These tools would enable you to communicate more effectively, and on a more personal level, with your past customers and to reward them for loyalty. CRM supports personalized promotions, e-mail campaigns, special customer events, etc. Loyalty systems reward frequent customers with something of value.	If your customers would benefit from regular communications from your business and would appreciate special offers, tailored to them, then CRM is a valuable tool. It is not worth investing in CRM if you don't already have EPOS and probably e-commerce in place as you won't have the past customer purchasing data from which to base your communications.
Planning tool	All aspects of planning. Some businesses choose to invest in a database-driven planning tool that automatically connects the range plan to WSSI, for instance. Others are quite comfortable developing their processes within tools such as Microsoft Excel. Excel is perfectly adequate – many *major* companies rely on using Excel to plan and monitor literally millions of pounds' worth of stock movements. I've seen *big* retailers planning entire seasons of purchase orders on spreadsheets – mainly because they're easy to use, flexible and cheap to implement!	You need to be planning even pre start-up, so this isn't really a choice! It's not a case of 'why consider it'; it's more a case of how much detail to build into the planning process at what level of evolution of your business. I would advocate developing robust processes *before* you really need them in place – this means when you move into a growth phase you've embedded the skills, behaviours, processes and systems and can upscale with relative ease!

TABLE 10.1 *continued*

Software solution type	Business processes supported	Why you should consider it
Stock management	Management of stock features in the business plan, WSSI and cash flow.	If you want to have a good view of your stock on hand and orders due you will need some kind of stock-management system. Typically this could be done as a report; if your orders are recorded into your accounting system (mentioned below) and your stock is booked into your EPOS on receipt, then you will have the data and this should be a case of drawing them together. If your systems are well implemented a good IT person could build a report that viewed SKU-level stock on hand, by location if you have several stores or a fulfilment operation, and stock on order. This will be important for both operational planning with WSSI and cash-flow management.

TABLE 10.1   *continued*

Software solution type	Business processes supported	Why you should consider it
Order tracking	Keeping track of orders supports supplier communications and appraisal. In addition this supports the stock-management processes (eg if due dates for an order change that will impact on WSSI stock and intake flow).	You need to have some visibility as to when stock on order will be received, as we discussed in Steps 8 and 9. You can do this with a simple spreadsheet, but bear in mind that if order due dates change this will need to be updated in the actual order document on your ordering system so that this can feed into the stock-management process. Late orders will impact WSSI and potentially cause you a future risk of an out-of-stock situation.
Collaboration	Information-sharing with suppliers and other third parties.	You might want to consider a collaboration tool if you have to liaise with third parties such as suppliers, designers or logistics providers as part of your regular business processes. Such tools are great for online meetings, sharing documents, working on projects remotely. If you think this would be something relevant to your business it would be worth looking at the different options for collaboration with remote third parties.

TABLE 10.1 *continued*

Software solution type	Business processes supported	Why you should consider it
Accounting	Business-critical financial processes, bookkeeping, statutory financial reporting, some aspects of stock management, recording of cash movements, purchase ordering, payroll.	This is another system that you almost have no choice about. You or your accountant will need to record your financial data in a system in order to produce your end-of-year accounts. In addition, as many of the statutory accounting and reporting processes can be done online, a system really speeds things up. An accounting system not only supports the critical business accounting requirements but can additionally enable you to access financial performance data and report on past income and expenditure. Hand-in-hand with EPOS and planning you *need* an accounting system of some sort!
Analytics/ reporting	Analytics and reporting underpin *all* business processes, so are a bit of an anomaly! You need to review performance in order to know what immediate and future actions to take to avoid problems and to improve in future. Typically, you won't need to buy a system just for analytics and reporting. Most systems will have some reporting built in, especially EPOS. However, there are software companies who sell tools that can do *all* of the list above and have solutions suitable for smaller businesses. These of course have the best reporting tools because the reports draw on the business data from all of the system processes.	

As mentioned before, there are so many different suppliers of software and solutions that it is easy to get confused and give up trying to work out who to choose altogether! My advice is to look at who in the market (and by this I mean *big* retailers) are doing things you want to be able to do: Amazon? ASOS? Tesco? Walmart? Hotel Chocolat? ToysRus? Marks & Spencer? John Lewis? White Company? Dreams? Boux Avenue? Identify with a few of those who you would aspire to replicate in terms of operating model, capability, service proposition, style, etc. Then identify software systems that will enable you to achieve the same. It doesn't have to be the same system that the big players use, but it will need to be able to deliver the same functionality. Remember: start with the end in mind. If you can design a solution that enables you to be what you want to be in future, not just to be what you already are, then you're onto a winner!

Finally, as we touched on in Step 8 regarding supplier selection, IT systems are a capital investment. Do plenty of research, work alongside an expert in systems and software implementations if this is an area that concerns you, and select your software supplier with care. Use your legal representative to check all the contracts, terms and service-level agreements as well – the last thing you need is an EPOS system to fail and a service-level agreement that states you could be waiting several days for it to be fixed.

Before we close this chapter, and indeed complete all of the 10 steps to retail success, I want to just look at how to include some of these four back-office areas into your business: considering outsourcing vs in-house.

Outsourcing vs in-house

One of the big decisions you need to make, and pretty early on in your planning, is how much of your business process to outsource and what to retain in-house. As a rule of thumb I'd be aiming in the mid to long term to definitely bring in-house any processes that could give you competitive advantage, and definitely outsource any processes that can be managed by your team but delivered to a consistent standard by a third party.

An example: you would not outsource product selection – you need that done by someone who is part of the fabric of the business, who understands the customer, the strategy, and is in daily communication with your suppliers. You could outsource deliveries. As long as there were clear quality guidelines and service agreements in place, a third party could undertake deliveries on your behalf.

In general I am an advocate of outsourcing – that is, having routine, non-business-critical tasks done by a third party. Paying someone who is an expert in 'getting the job done' may cost a little more than the equivalent employment but it removes a great deal of risk too. You don't need to worry about sickness and holiday cover, for instance, when you outsource. With the right partners you will get a higher quality, more consistent and more reliable outcome.

In the early days this would also apply to HR, legal, finance and IT but ultimately you should ensure that you bring most of the core back-office skills (possibly with the exception of legal advice and accountancy review) back in-house at some point. As you grow you should plan to have a dedicated HR manager, finance manager and IT manager – they will be able to take all of the back-office processes off your hands, be your internal experts in each of their functional areas, and manage all of the day-to-day issues and third-party relationships. By having this team in-house you will find that instead of trying to do everything yourself and through liaison with external third parties, you are spending more time leading the business and less time trying to do four people's jobs!

Summing up

Congratulations for completing the tenth and final step in the 10 steps to retail success process!

In this chapter we covered four back-office aspects that really ensure your business operates like a well-oiled machine.

We have talked about the importance of

- Human Resources: planning the organizational structure, managing the resources and making sure you have clear policies in place;
- Legal: keeping an eye on all your commercial agreements to avoid risk or penalty in the future, protecting your brand;
- Finance: ensuring your business is compliant with all the financial reporting obligations and taxation requirements, being as efficient and profitable as possible;
- IT: delivering relevant, appropriate business information and transactional systems that enable consumers to buy from you with ease and having access to data so that you can manage your business effectively.

Finally we looked at outsourcing vs in-house for each of these areas. So, now you should have a good understanding of the areas you need to improve on in your back office, and how best to engage the support.

That's it. Congratulations! That's the end of the 10 steps to success process. The final chapter is a short conclusion, a brief review of all the steps, and a reminder about the importance of implementing your action plan! Now you've got all the actions listed you can develop robust and repeatable processes and systems. Are you ready to commit to making *your* retail business a scalable, saleable enterprise?

If so, turn the page...

Conclusion

Well done! You have reached the end of the 10 steps to retail success process. I'm only going to give a very brief reminder of how to turn everything we've covered into your own action plan. I am sure that rather than spend time discussing it you'll want to get started on it right away!

In the Introduction I said:

> The aim of this book is to help more retail business owners, whether starting up or already trading, online only or multi-channel, to develop robust and repeatable processes and systems to create scalable, saleable enterprises.

Now you've completed the 10 steps to retail success this is the beginning of your journey to reach your goals. Some clients have worked through the steps with me as a part of a programme, spanning six or 12 months. Together we take time to complete a whole review of their business, step by step, and to implement more rigorous processes and systems around each step as we go. I have found that for many clients they don't need to do too much in some areas but have quite a lot to do in others – typically where the business owner has least interest or expertise! That of course is perfectly normal and to be expected.

This approach can be used over and over again as your business develops, and at each iteration you'll be improving your business and your processes, developing and building on the last time you worked through it. Using the 10 steps to retail success methodology should be a continuous improvement process – you will need to regularly review your business; every business owner should. One of the key statements I made in the Introduction was that to avoid being a victim of economic conditions and shifts in consumer behaviour you need to constantly re-evaluate your business model and revise it where appropriate. You should be asking yourself: Is the offer still relevant? Am I moving with the times? You don't want to get left behind.

Throughout the 10 steps we've covered ways to develop and embed robust and repeatable processes and systems and explained how this will enable you to become a scalable, saleable business. Therefore, I hope you will agree, we have achieved the aim of the book. Achieving *your* aims will come down to what actions *you* choose to take now, and as a result of reading this book.

Right at the beginning I introduced the 10 steps to retail success self-appraisal tool. I suggested that you use the self-appraisal tool and complete the 'current position' column. As we worked through each chapter I hope you made some notes regarding what your target position should be, but if you didn't, make sure you do it now. You should also make notes of the actions that you have identified that you will need to complete in order to achieve your target position. With these elements you should have a comprehensive action plan.

Now it's time to review what you've noted, add prioritization based on what seems most appropriate for your business, and set yourself some realistic dates for when you'll have completed the actions. Some of the actions may be dependent on other actions having been done – in which case you can make a note in the priority column if there is a dependency on another action having first been completed.

If you'd rather not write directly into the table below you can either re-create this form in your own style (with your own additional columns if you wish) or you can download this template via **www.retailchampion.co.uk/ resources** – it's called '10-steps to retail success self-appraisal'.

Once all the pieces are in place you've got the template for success. You know where you are, where you want to be, how to get there and have a prioritized action plan to help you achieve it.

If you have done this alone, without the support of a mentor or advisor to keep you on track, you could fall into the trap of having a great plan in place but never actually getting around to implementing it. That would mean you make no progress whatsoever! If you know that you are the sort of person who needs a bit of external support, the occasional 'push' and, to put it bluntly, someone to nag you from time to time, then find someone who you can assign to do just that! Someone you trust, someone who is involved in your business but not entrenched in the day-to-day: a business advisor, accountant, HR expert or even another business owner. What you have to do to assign your 'nag' is simply share the plans you have with them and ask them to chase you up on the action list to make sure you stay on track. You can do the same for them if they are also in business. This kind of support won't quite replace a mentor/coach or advisor, but it will certainly make quite a difference to you if you 'externalize' the plan and feel account-able to an independent third party whose duty is to check up on you!

I hope that you have enjoyed working through the 10 steps to retail success as much as I have enjoyed sharing them.

I have one last thing to share; maybe I've saved the best until last! It's an interview with Mike Clare, Founder of Dreams, who kindly wrote the Foreword to this book. Mike shares his memories of what it was like for him when he started Dreams, what kept him going, and how he felt at various stages of his business growth.

If for one moment you think that you will never become the owner of the next *big* retail chain, look back on this story – Mike started out with just one store. His personal wealth is a result of his hard work, dedication, determination, passion and enormous self-belief. In the early days he strug-gled for cash just like any start-up. Mike is a lovely guy, successful and engaging but he is *not* unique. If he can do it, you can too.

TABLE C.1 You are now ready to complete your 10 steps to retail success self-appraisal tool

Step and short description	Current position	Target position	Actions required	Dependent actions	Priority: H/M/L	Cost estimate	Due date
1. Goal and mission: Has clearly defined goal and mission statement							
2. Positioning: Has determined positioning in respect of product, price, presentation and service							
3. Ideal customer: Has clearly documented ideal customer for each range planned							
4. Range planning: Has a clear documented approach to range construction, width vs depth and it matches the mission, positioning and customer needs							
5. Pricing and promotions: Has a price architecture, price ladder and promotional approach that fit with positioning							
6. Channel and location: Has determined the routes to market in line with ideal customer expectations							

TABLE C.1 *continued*

Step and short description	Current position	Target position	Actions required	Dependent actions	Priority: H/M/L	Cost estimate	Due date
7. Customer engagement: Has PR and marketing plan, social engagement strategy and processes for customer attraction, conversion and retention							
8. Supply chain: Knows where products will be sourced, what supplier relationship management process is and has defined logistics processes							
9. Planning and controlling: Has documented plans for range, buying, costing, stock flow, cash flow and uses them to control and monitor the business							
10. Back office (HR, Legal, Fi and IT): Has determined organizational structure and resourcing plan, sourced appropriate professional services (Legal, Finance) and has a clear IT roadmap in place							

A dream come true... interview with Mike Clare, Founder and President of Dreams plc

"Looking back, right at the beginning, it was really nerve-racking starting a business! I had to consider my wife, our first child on the way, our home, the bank, and of course, my own pride – all on the line! There was a lot at stake!

When I recruited my first employee it was exhilarating; but also a huge sense of responsibility. I had the constant thought in the back of my mind: 'I'd better not mess this up!'

The money to get started came in part from finance and in part from savings. I originally had only £2k in savings, so I downgraded my MGB for an Avenger (£2k) raised money (£5k) on my credit card (for a 'fictional' new kitchen) and then the rest came from Lloyds Bank who matched my 'total savings' – £9k × 2 = £18k – that was my start-up fund.

The whole thing was a little scary but it was also what drove me on. I had my family, the bank and my customers relying on me – so I had no choice, it just had to work! I wanted to be a success and I had gut feeling this was going to work. I have always been competitive (my biggest rival as a child was my brother) so failure wasn't an option; I would never give up.

There were lots of great moments...

- when I got the keys to my first shop;
- building a great team who became colleagues and friends;
- winning 'Furniture Retailer of the Year' (a record three times!);
- right through to the sale process in 2008 (good times!).

There were ups and downs, of course, but I wouldn't change a thing.

I believed I was always going to be successful. Cocky or confident? It's a fine line! There were many sacrifices that my wife, my children and I made to create the success. It looks easy in hindsight, but in reality it's a lot to do with bloody hard work! As a family we now have lots of fun together! My wife and I travel the world, I'm involved with many charities and other investments, as well as Dreams.

In my view, retailing is all about what I call the 3 × Ps – Passion, People and Perseverance. Find something you're 'Passionate' about, do your homework, find out what it is that you can do that's unique and different, focus on one thing and be the best at it. Once you've done that, it's all about your team, your 'People'. Find the best, pay a little more than the industry average – you'll get twice as good. Finally, you've got to have 'Perseverance'. Things will go wrong and you will get that 'door slammed in your face' but whatever you do, never ever give up on your Dreams!

Even when the going gets tough, keep the passion alive, make sure you have the best team, and persevere no matter what.

Even though Dreams was sold in 2008, because I'm an entrepreneur it's in my blood to keep going! My wife, Carol, and I took a year out after the sale of Dreams and went round the world but we quickly got bored! So we decided to get into something we've always had a passion for but never had the time for – 'unusual properties'. We set up Amazing Retreats, which takes a lot of my time.

We also wanted to 'give something back' so we set up The Clare Foundation, a charity helping other charities to become more commercial and efficient. So, Carol and I are still very busy and enjoying life to the max!"

It was great to speak to Mike about the early days of Dreams, he was so animated and there was no doubt that every word he said he passionately believed in.

Perhaps one day I'll be interviewing you after you have sold your retail empire and you'll be sharing your story for the next generation of retailers to take inspiration from.

Until then, I hope that all *your* Dreams come true for *your* retail business. To your success.

Clare Rayner

APPENDIX

The Retail Champion

The Retail Champion – mission

The Retail Champion offers **retail expertise and bespoke business mentoring programmes** to business owners who are either retailers or suppliers to retail. Retailers will **develop robust and repeatable processes and systems;** suppliers to retail will create a compelling value proposition and go-to-market strategy. The Retail Champion enables *all* clients to **become scalable, saleable businesses.**

How The Retail Champion can help you!

The Retail Champion mentoring programmes can be tailored to provide you with mentoring, advice, support, consultancy, project management and training. Clients comment that the advice, support, guidance and expertise delivered by The Retail Champion have been invaluable to their businesses.

Typically, clients are smaller, independent retailers or suppliers to retail. The reasons clients give for choosing to work with The Retail Champion are lack of time, lack of retail expertise or lack of confidence in making tough decisions to really drive their businesses forward on their own. So The Retail Champion fills the gaps by:

- keeping you on track, **focusing your time** on the value-added activities that achieve your business aims and objectives;

- **sharing expertise** and helping you to develop strategies to increase profit, customer base, revenue streams and channels to market;

- acting as a sounding board for your ideas, providing feedback and validation from an expert third party to **give you the confidence that you are making the right choices!**

Mentoring programmes on a one-to-one basis with The Retail Champion are offered to a maximum of 10 non-competing businesses at any point in time. These businesses benefit from working hand-in-hand with Clare Rayner. Your programme is uniquely tailored to your needs and includes regular contact (face-to-face, e-mail, phone, webinar) so that your business

can benefit from working with one of the UK's most well-known retail experts without breaking the bank.
www.retailchampion.co.uk

The Retail Conference

The Retail Conference – mission

The Retail Conference is the UK's leading retail industry forum for senior decision makers and those who define business strategy in the retail sector to meet, network and share their success stories. Delivered by retailers, for retailers, hosted in a quality venue with exceptional catering and facilities, this is a not-to-be-missed event. All attendees should expect a very worthwhile and informative day away from the office.

About The Retail Conference

The Retail Conference, which is organized by Retail Acumen, was first delivered in 2007 and fast became the UK's leading conference for senior decision makers and those who define business strategy in the retail sector. The format encompasses keynote seminars, breakout sessions and workshops, panel discussion and plenty of networking time.

The content is focused on real-life case studies, industry insights, examples of best practice in action and thought leadership. The event provides an engaging and inspiring learning experience for all those who attend. Uniquely, the content is focused on what really matters to retailers; topical, relevant and forward-looking.

The Retail Conference is different from other events for three key reasons:

- It was the first true conference-format event to offer *free* attendance to retailers. Many have tried to follow, few have had the sustainable growth and success of The Retail Conference.

- All keynote speakers are guaranteed to be either experienced retail practitioners or representatives of best-practice organizations. Sponsors only ever take to the stage when supporting their retail client.

- Being a content-centric event there is only ever one sponsor presenting on their core expertise. Sponsors are selected for their quality, credibility, proven track record and innovative concepts. Retailers can have confidence that if they want to take their conversations with the sponsors further they are speaking to genuine industry experts.

When delegates attend The Retail Conference they benefit from:

- hearing success stories from engaging speakers who are guaranteed to be either retailers or leading experts in a highly topical field;
- expanding their knowledge through topical workshops and breakout sessions;
- debating a hot topic with expert panellists in the panel discussion;
- gaining an insight into what other retailers are doing, with real-world case studies;
- networking time with other retailers, sharing experiences, issues and challenges;
- taking time out to focus on what really matters to them in their business;
- renewed passion and enthusiasm and some great new ideas to put into practice!

www.retailconference.co.uk

Retail Acumen

Retail Acumen – mission

Retail Acumen delivers deep, detailed analysis and insights into business performance for retail multiples. Our specialist team leverage their love of detailed data analytics, combined with a deep understanding of the retail sector, to uncover practical, easily implementable, optimization opportunities. Our clients benefit from recommendations that identify simple business change that will achieve maximum performance improvement, fast.

Retail Acumen – services

No professional can be expected to take a business decision with confidence without evidence to back it up. At Retail Acumen it is our job to arm decision makers with the information they need to confidently proceed with changes that will significantly improve business performance in four key areas to:

- **increase sales.** In addition to having product available on the shelf, clearly labelled, and helpful well-trained sales staff, it is critical that retailers analyse their operational performance at store level. Retail Acumen's increase-sales process measures relative store (and website) performance for metrics such as footfall/traffic, conversion rate and

ATV, in order to assist clients in understanding the operational dynamics and spread of performance across the chain. This insight enables further action to enhance performance ongoing.

- **intensify assortment.** Every SKU in your range should earn its right to be there. If it's not contributing to the bottom line then it is adding unnecessary management overhead and stockholding costs. Retail Acumen's range rationalization process measures relative SKU contribution for metrics such as sales and margin; often under 10 per cent of SKUs deliver 80 per cent of cash margin! We model the impact of culling underperforming SKUs; creating a proposal for a reduced range that considers both range architecture and price ladder. The outcome is a sensible discontinuation list, based not only on the numbers but also on the value each SKU adds to your range.

- **improve return on space.** The nuances of performance at store level are the key to unlocking more profit from retail space. Retail Acumen's return-on-space analytics measure relative return on space considering both cost and margin, per unit of space, for each store uniquely. By understanding the spread of performance across the chain, the worst performers can be targeted and improvement actions put in place.

- **optimize supply chain.** Effective supply-chain management enables an efficient, cost-effective flow of stock. Often, when SKU-store stock levels are analysed, maldistribution – indicative of a suboptimal supply chain – is observed. Retail Acumen's supply-chain optimization process measures relative SKU-store stock levels compared to the ideal. This analysis highlights the risks of lost sales and stock obsolescence due to maldistribution, even when the sum of store stock levels meets company targets. Further investigation identifies causal factors that impact on stock levels. The outcome is an action plan to reduce maldistribution in future.

e-mphasis Internet Marketing

e-mphasis Internet Marketing – mission

e-mphasis Internet Marketing is the supplier of choice for delivery of local search marketing, multi-channel search marketing and mobile search marketing for businesses who serve the consumer (retail, hospitality and leisure). e-mphasis's expert and innovative team consistently deliver exceptional, measurable and repeatable results so clients benefit from incremental sales and impressive ROI.

About e-mphasis Internet Marketing

e-mphasis Internet Marketing is a digital marketing agency that specializes in providing a range of relevant, appropriate search marketing services to clients whose customers are consumers – specifically those in retail, hospitality and leisure.

e-mphasis was founded by Andrew Rayner, a search marketing expert, who has been working with internet-related technologies since the internet came into existence in 1996. Andrew and the team at e-mphasis have developed innovative search marketing techniques to enable clients to get found online for their desired search terms. This increases the volume of relevant search traffic, which in turn has led clients to report uplifted sales that represent up to 30 times return on investment within just one year of engaging e-mphasis services!

e-mphasis offers search engine optimization, multi-channel search marketing, and has developed a unique local internet marketing service which is particularly effective for mobile search marketing and event-based marketing. As a result of their focus on local search, e-mphasis are now considered to be the leading local search marketing experts in the UK.

www.e-mphasis.com

About Mike Clare

Biography for Mike Clare, Executive Chairman – Clarenco

Mike was born and bred in Beaconsfield so becoming a Deputy Lieutenant and a 'Buckinghamshire Ambassador' makes him especially proud of his Buckinghamshire involvements and heritage. Nowadays, Mike lives in the Buckinghamshire Chiltern countryside with his wife Carol and family. Mike was educated at Davenies School, Chalfont's Community College and High Wycombe College (now BNU) before starting a career in the retail furniture industry, which ultimately led to him opening his own bed store at the age of 30.

Although a serial entrepreneur, Mike is probably best known as the founder of Dreams, which he launched with one store in 1987, growing to over 250 superstores before Mike eventually stepped down as chairman and CEO in 2008, although he still remains involved as a major shareholder and non-executive president.

Mike realized he wasn't quite ready for retirement in 2008 so he decided to pursue his love of unique and iconic properties, making a hobby into a business. Mike has now built up a considerable property portfolio through Clarenco LLP: not only conventional commercial and residential property (in Buckinghamshire, of course) but also amazing and unusual properties such as towers, castles, forts and monasteries (throughout Britain) under the Amazing Retreat brand.

Mike also has many philanthropic interests including The Prince's Trust, The Retail Trust, Worshipful Company of Furniture Makers, Wycombe 4C and, of course, his own charity, The Clare Foundation, which he conceived and started in 2009. Their aim is to support and improve the efficiency of charities throughout the UK and help them become more commercial and entrepreneurial. Based in Saunderton, near High Wycombe, The Clare Foundation also acts as a hub for local Buckinghamshire charities by offering subsidized accommodation and shared resources.

Mike also finds time to help and mentor many local businesses and entrepreneurs and is often heard on the speaker circuit, lecturing and advising students and businessmen alike, guiding them along the path of success and helping make their dreams come true.

Mike is a Freeman of the City of London, a Fellow of the Institute of Directors and a winner of numerous entrepreneurial awards. In 2009 Mike was awarded an Honorary Doctorate by Bucks New University in recognition of his outstanding achievements in the field of commerce and entrepreneurship.

INDEX

NB: page numbers in *italic* indicate figures or tables
chapter summaries are indexed as summaries of chapters